The Promise of Obedience:

A Ritual History

Leon F. Strieder

The Promise of Obedience:

A Ritual History

A PUEBLO BOOK

The Liturgical Press Collegeville, Minnesota

A Pueblo Book published by The Liturgical Press

Design by Frank Kacmarcik, Obl.S.B. Illustration: Caeremoniale Episcoporum, Clementis VIII, ARCA ARTIUM.

Library of Congress Cataloging-in-Publication Data

Strieder, Leon, 1950–
    The promise of obedience : a ritual history / Leon Strieder.
      p. cm.
    "A Pueblo book."
    Includes bibliographical references and index.
    ISBN 0-8146-6016-9 (alk. paper)
    1. Ordination—Catholic Church—History. 2. Catholic Church—
Liturgy—History. 3. Obedience, Vow of. I. Title.

BX2240 .S77 2001
264'.20284'09—dc21   2001029890

Contents

Preface

Upon hearing that in revisions of the 1990 second typical edition for the rites of ordinations there had been added a promise of obedience to the local diocesan bishop for religious deacons and presbyters, the seed was planted in my mind that it would be helpful to study not only the rationale for this addition but indeed the entire history of promises of obedience in ordination rites. When the opportunity came that I would be able to do the doctorate in sacred liturgy, I began some serious preliminary reading on the topic. Thus I arrived at the doors of San Anselmo with a fairly clear understanding of the questions that needed to be asked and the historical method that needed to be followed. This work, then, is essentially my doctoral dissertation from the Pontifical Liturgical Institute of San Anselmo in Rome. I am most appreciative to Fr. Anscar Chupungco, O.S.B., for his willingness to work with me on this topic and for his insightful and gentle guidance as the work progressed.

Due to the relational and reciprocal nature of obedience, the major questions needed to be centered on the relationship between the parties involved in any promise of obedience; namely, the one making the promise and the one to whom the promise is made. This would include an understanding of the historical context of each rite and promise, but without imposing modern concerns on a previous period of history. It would likewise include an understanding of the theological context in which any rite or promise in ordination rites would be developed. Finally, it would include an understanding of the canonical or juridical context of ordained ministry as these relationships were lived out over the centuries. These three contexts are precedent to and implicit in any ritual expression and, in particular, in any ritual expression of obedience.

The historical method that needed to be followed was quite easy to ascertain. Since the first time we find a promise of obedience in rites of ordination is in the tenth-century Romano-Germanic Pontifical, chapter 1 is a historical introduction that gives the historical background, tracing the origin and development of the promise of obedience and its ritual connection with the bestowal of the pallium. The key historical personage here is Boniface, and the central ecclesial issue is the freeing of the Church in the face of local lords and proprietary churches.

Chapter 2 details the development of the promise of obedience in ordination rites in the pontificals up through Trent. Using the principles of the comparative method of textual analysis, we follow the development of the promise of obedience in ordination rites and question the rationale for each change. What is key here is the freedom with which the various compilers moved the promise of obedience within the various rites. This forms the heart of our study.

Due to the reciprocal relationship between promises of obedience in ordination rites and those in monastic and mendicant rites of profession and the blessing of abbots, chapter 3 is a study of that relationship. Beginning with Benedict and following the same historical and comparative method of textual analysis, we are able to show that monastic and mendicant rites have had a rich influence, both theological and ritual, on the promises of obedience in ordination rites.

Chapter 4 studies the issues and textual developments of the Second Vatican Council concerning promises of obedience in ordination rites. In particular, we have the movement toward a ritual and theological symmetry in which now all three rites of ordination—bishop, presbyter, and deacon—contain similar ritual examinations with promises of obedience immediately prior to the actual ordination. Theologically, the key issues concern the understanding of the relationships between bishops and the pope and between bishops and presbyters and deacons in the light of the teachings of the Second Vatican Council.

Chapter 5 studies the revisions of the 1990 second typical edition, and because of its recent event, forms a timely section. It is timely because the various episcopal conferences and episcopal committees responsible for the various language groups must prepare both translations and adaptations for their respective constituencies. Theologically it is timely because the ritual developments of a promise of obedience for religious presbyters and deacons to the local diocesan

bishop is a most significant statement regarding the future development of the understanding of religious who also share in holy orders.
We are most grateful to Professor Reiner Kaczynski for his timely help
and documentation of this most recent development.

Chapter 6 is a study of the Eastern rites and Eastern Catholic
churches to recognize their importance in any further development in
the ecclesial understanding of ordained ministry for the entire Catholic Church. The key issues here concern the theological and canonical
developments in the understanding of the patriarchal and metropolitan structures of the Eastern churches.

The strengths of this study, it would seem, are twofold. First, as we
mentioned, is its timeliness with regard to the work of translation and
adaptation, which now must occur after the revisions of the second
typical edition of the rites of ordination. It is hoped that the questions
asked of the texts proposed for our time will be of help for those who
must continue the ongoing task of inculturation. Second, it is hoped
that the compilation of all the major texts that concern the development of the promise of obedience in ordination rites will be a usable
tool for anyone who would wish to know its historical and ritual story.

The weaknesses of this study lie mainly in the fact that this is a ritual, liturgical study, and thus many of the theological and canonical
questions remain to be answered, leaving many issues to be resolved.
It is hoped that perhaps this work will aid in a decision by those in
the related fields of theology and canon law to do just such work.

Roman Beginnings and the Pallium

As with all things Christian, one must begin with Christ, and when one thinks of obedience in the Christian context, the text of the liturgical hymn in Philippians comes immediately to mind. Here we are told that our attitude must be that of Christ, who "humbled himself, obediently accepting even death, death on a cross!" (2:8). This text, sung by the earliest of Christians, puts the essence of Christ's salvific mission in the context of his obedience to the will of his Father. More importantly, it is the context of the eternal Logos expressing and responding to the will of the Father. This is the philological dynamism of the concept of obedience. In Greek, as our scriptural context gives us, ὑπήκοος (hupikoos), as well as the Latin cognate of our English word, obedience means to listen to and submit oneself to the word of another. It is a relational term implying two persons, one speaking and another listening. Our comprehension of this dynamism is essential for any understanding of the incarnation, and thus it is central to any understanding of what it means to have our attitude be that of Christ and to obediently accept our cross. Thus discipleship demands obedience to the master, and it flows out of the very core of our relationship with Christ. This relational dynamism of obedience is one of the keys to keep in mind as we work through the rituals that celebrate it in our history.

The second set of introductory remarks must deal with a correct understanding of the development of both the various rituals and the texts that describe them.

First, we must speak of culture.[1] Every ritual action has its proper cultural context. Culture is often understood in its very limited definition

---

[1] Chupungco, *Liturgical Inculturation: Sacramentals, Religiosity, and Catechesis,* 35–37. See also Power, *The Eucharistic Mystery: Rivitalizing the Tradition,* 6–16.

as an acquired appreciation, development, or refinement of the mind, morals, or taste. More basic to our work and to the meaning of the word, culture is the construct upon which all human understanding and relationships are built in any given context. Intrinsic here are the temporal and spatial concepts that mark any human group, and more importantly, here also are the relational concepts of family, society, authority, and order. Finally, within these relational concepts are the more abstract human virtues such as trust, love, and forgiveness. While all these items are common to all peoples and to all times, the particulars as to their understanding differ for each people and each time.

This issue is primary for understanding the many layers of ritual expression already present in the Judaism of Jesus' time, the early Christian synthesis of Jewish and Hellenistic cultures, and the further amalgamation of these in the Roman culture with its rich legal heritage.

We must keep in tension the various cultures and the historical development of the liturgical books pertinent to any ritual study.[2] We can track liturgical texts from Rome to the land of the Franks and then back again to Rome. This is level 1. Level 2 includes the movement from Rome to Avignon and back again to Rome. Finally, level 3, since Trent and especially in our times, involves the movement from Rome to the entire Latin Church and back again as we continue to struggle with issues of inculturation. In essence, no ritual text is pure. It is the result of much cultural development and textual interplay as certain writers copy and adapt certain texts, which have their own context, and certain peoples struggle to make those texts their own. This is the essential difference between a celebration of the faith of a particular people and the texts that may mark that celebration. Finally, historical contexts and political purposes must be viewed in the positive light of how the Holy Spirit guides the Church. Any lesser understanding will throw our study into ideological battles that are not helpful.

A final set of introductory remarks must deal with the nature of textual development. The ritual texts as we have them today are basically conservative; that is, they are the result of the desire to codify and preserve what is already present in any faith tradition. Thus any text from the eighth or tenth century includes material far older than

---

[2] These ideas are well summarized by Vogel, *Medieval Liturgy: An Introduction to the Sources*, 3.

that century. This, plus the natural desire to simply include previous texts, has preserved for us some very ancient texts.

Much more important is an understanding that some textual compilers imposed certain theological and sometimes ideological purposes on a text. While it is difficult to ascertain all the levels of meaning in a text, with the aid of good historical analysis we can recognize some of these purposes and deal with them accordingly. Again, we must view this in the broader light of the Holy Spirit guiding the Church.

Finally, we must say a word about false texts, which, unknown to the compilers of later texts, simply were copied as if they were long-standing traditions. One example is the False Decretals, attributed to a fictitious Isidore Mercator, which nevertheless had a tremendous influence in the Church at large and which ended up as part of Gratian's Decretals some three hundred years later as long-standing teachings of the Church.

ROMAN BEGINNINGS

While the first ordination rites to contain promises of obedience for both bishops and presbyters are found in the Romano-Germanic Pontifical of the tenth century, we must search for the roots of such promises in a much earlier time. Long before this pontifical, and as a prelude for Charlemagne, we have the person of Boniface, who is the great bridge between Rome and the kingdom of the Franks. It was Boniface who, on November 30, 722, was consecrated bishop by Pope Gregory II and who took the promise of obedience the suffragan bishops of the Roman province made to the Pope.[3] At this point we make the historical connection and state that the wording of the promise of obedience in the Romano-Germanic Pontifical is based on the wording of this Roman promise of obedience. This is level 1 in our textual evolution; that is, something Roman takes on a Frankish context.

The other element we find in Boniface is the bestowal of the pallium and the authority it signifies. In 732 Pope Gregory III raised Boniface to archbishop and bestowed upon him the pallium.[4] While the pallium seems to have a pagan, Oriental origin and was part of the normal vestiture of the Roman emperor, we have some archaeological

---

[3] E. Ewig in Jedin, *Handbook of Church History,* 3:11.
[4] Ibid., 12.

documentation that it was part of the various elements of vestment that some church leaders wore from the fourth century on.[5] Seen as a sign of authority to rule, it was also understood as a sign that gave one authority to delegate by sending others in his name and later will be seen as part of the authority to ordain suffragan bishops. It seems that from the fourth century on, the pallium was a part of the office of the bishop of Rome. This simple beginning developed into a significant rite symbolizing the power of the Bishop of Rome and the obedience owed him by his suffragan bishops, and later, by archbishops and metropolitans.

First, looking at this rite of the bestowing of the pallium, we see that the early rites were exceedingly simple. Ordo XL A, which is a sixth-century rite for the ordination of the Roman pontiff, already has the three major suffragan bishops involved in this rite.

"The bishop of Albano gives the first prayer. Then the bishop of Portus gives the second prayer. After that the book of the Gospels is brought and held open over the head of the elect by the deacons. Then the bishop of Ostia consecrates him pontiff. After this the archdeacon places the pallium on him. Then he ascends to his chair and gives the kiss of peace to all the priests and says *Gloria in excelsis Deo.*"[6]

In this early text it is the bishop of Ostia who has the honor of consecrating the pontiff. We should point out the unique ecclesiology of Rome, and indeed the entire early Church, which had its bishop elected from among the ranks of the clergy there, especially the deacons, who were very powerful in Rome.[7] This is also part of the theological concept of the bishop as wed to his diocese, a concept that did not allow for bishops to be transferred to another diocese. In the above rite the archdeacon places the pallium on the shoulders of the pontiff, who then goes to his chair and gives all the priests a kiss of peace. It would seem that "priests" here means both presbyters and bishops. In later centuries this kiss of peace will take on a rather opposite form, one that would symbolize submission to the pontiff. This

---

[5] Salmon, *Etude sur Les Insignes du Pontife dans Le Rit Romain,* 21–2.

[6] M. Andrieu, *Les Ordines romani du haut moyen âge,* 4:294–7.

[7] For a thorough study see M. Andrieu, "La carrière ecclésiastique des Papes et les documents liturgiques du Moyen Âge," 91–120.

text is basically repeated in Ordo XXXVI, a ninth-century text,[8] and Ordo XL B, a tenth-century text.[9]

Returning to the second element of the pallium, namely the power to delegate, we find a rich early history of papal vicariates. These mainly concerned the two sees of Seville and Arles, were often very specific in nature, did not at first include the bestowal of a pallium, and lasted only for the duration of the pontificate. The purpose of the vicariate was to protect the interests of the Bishop of Rome in the local church.

Zeno of Seville was the first to have full authority, conferred upon him by Pope Simplicius (468–83) to protect papal interests in Spain. The vicariate of Arles dates from the time of Pope Zosimus (417–18) and was reconfirmed by Leo the Great (440–61). The first bestowal of the pallium occurred in 513, when Pope Symmachus (498–514) gave Caesarius of Arles the pallium *at the invitation of the pontiff* as his vicar for the Gallic and Spanish provinces. Here we find the first connection between a vicariate and the pallium.

Pope Gregory I (590–604) sent a pallium to Leander of Seville, but here the pallium took on the sign of a personal honor, since at this time the historical situation in Spain had changed and the interests of Rome were adequately protected by the local kings.[10] In fact, Gregory made great use of the pallium. Most famous was his sending of Augustine to Canterbury with the pallium as his vicar for England, but actually Gregory sent palliums to the metropolitans of thirteen sees, among them Milan, Ravenna, Corinth, and Palermo.[11] We see the beginnings of papal authority asserting itself in the sending of these palliums as symbols that these bishops were vicars, in some sense, of the Bishop of Rome. Yet this never usurped the authority and apostolicity of the local bishop.

BONIFACE AND THE EIGHTH CENTURY

To understand this great apostle of the Franks we have to acknowledge his roots. He was an Englishman named Winfrid who, along with a mandate to evangelize the Franks, was given the name Boniface

[8] Andrieu, *Les Ordines romani*, 4:203.

[9] Ibid., 308.

[10] H. J. Vogt in Jedin, *Handbook of Church History*, 2:636–8.

[11] Braun, *Die liturgische Gewandung in Occident und Orient nach Ursprung und Entwicklung, Verwendung und Symbolik*, 625.

by Pope Gregory II in 719. The English structure of church order was rather ultramontane, to use a term from another time. Augustine had arrived at Canterbury a century earlier with pallium and papal authority. The English-Irish church system at this time was founded on abbey-bishoprics. While this system had its weak points, such as using *chorepiscopi* for ordinations,[12] it allowed for a church independent of the local rulers. This was Boniface's experience of church authority.

In the kingdom of the Franks things were quite different. The system of proprietary churches was common there, and this was true as well in Visigothic Spain and Gaul. This system basically put the churches under the ownership of the local lords, who had presbyters under their vassalage to care for those churches. Likewise, territorial bishops owed their allegiance to the king. Boniface confronted this situation by founding abbey-bishoprics, similar to the English-Irish system of churches. This allowed many of the churches and their presbyters to be free from the local lord by being subject to the local abbey-bishopric. This gave these Frankish churches a Roman tradition, which allowed them to be loyal to Rome while many of the territorial bishops were obliged to the local lord.[13] While this system had its flaws, it allowed for much freedom for the local churches, presbyters, and bishops to be church and do what they were ordained to do. The promises of obedience played an important structural role in the lives of those bishops and presbyters.

Boniface's promise of obedience, as we stated above, was the promise taken by suffragan bishops at Rome. However, the obligation of loyalty to the emperor was replaced by the engagement not to be in communion with those bishops who acted against the Bishop of Rome, *against the ancient institutions of the holy Fathers,* and to take action against them or at least to report them to the pope.[14] It is obvious that Boniface's mission was intimately linked to Rome.

"I Boniface, bishop by the grace of God, promise *(Promitto ego Bonifacius)* to you blessed Peter, prince of the apostles, and to your vicar, blessed Pope Gregory, and his successors, through the Father, Son and Holy Spirit, the inseparable Trinity, and before your most holy body,

[12] Ryan,"The Legacy of the Schoolmen," 14–6.
[13] Knowles, *The Christian Centuries,* 2:11–54.
[14] E. Ewig in Jedin, *Handbook of Church History,* 3:11–2.

that I will exhibit complete fidelity and purity to the holy catholic faith *(me omnem fidem et puritatem sanctae fidei catholicae exhibere)*. . . .

"For the good of the church, as I said, I promise to you, to whom the power to bind and loose was given by the Lord God, and to his afore-mentioned vicar and his successors to exhibit in all things *(cui a Domino Deo potestas ligandi solvendique data est, et praedicto vicario tuo atque successoribus ejus, per omnia exhibere)* my fidelity and my purity *(fidem et puritatem meam)*.

"But if I know any bishops who have turned against the ancient insti-tutions of the holy Fathers *(contra instituta antiqua sanctorum Patrum)*, I will have nothing to do with them. What is more, if I can prohibit what they do, I will prohibit it. But at least, remaining faithful, I will renounce them to my Lord, the Pope. . . .

"Therefore I, Boniface, a minor bishop, have written this text of an oath *(indiculum sacramenti)* by my own hand, and placing it upon the most holy body of holy Peter *(ponens supra sacratissimum corpus sancti Petri)*, as it is prescribed, and with God as my witness, I have made an oath which I promise to preserve *(feci sacramentum, quod et conservare promitto)*."[15]

It was made upon the altar at St. Peter's, and indeed, is addressed to him and to his vicar, Gregory, and his successors. The first point we must make is that the altar of St. Peter's, built over the believed site of his bones, is a sacred place that in a real way represents his presence. This promise mentions Peter as if he were truly present. The text states that Boniface places the written promise, here called an oath *(sacramentum)*, upon the most holy body of holy Peter. In later texts that deal with promises, in particular monastic promises, we will note the use of the altar and the mention of the relics there. While later texts will not use the term *sacramentum* for such a promise, it is a term rich with symbolism for the deeper realities of one's commitment to the Lord and the Church.

Second, it is a personal promise, as it begins "I Boniface promise," and in the text he tells us that it was written in his own hand. The use of the term "I promise" forms one early tradition in which the person making the promise speaks from his own will, stating that he will do

[15] Migne, *Patrologiae Cursus Completus, series Latina*, 89:803–4.

what he promises. This is in contrast to a second tradition, in which the person is asked if he will do what is promised, the "Will you–I will" *(Vis-Volo)* structure, which is still in use today in our rites of ordination. The promise is made to another person, here "to you blessed Peter, prince of the apostles, and to your vicar, blessed Pope Gregory, and his successors." This is part of the relational nature of obedience. The promise is made from one person to another and his vicars and successors. It crosses time and structures but binds the persons involved. We make note of the title of Gregory as vicar of Peter. This is one of the most ancient titles of the Bishop of Rome. Finally, this personal promise by its nature demands that the person make it freely. The promise closes with Boniface restating that "I have made an oath which I promise to preserve."

The one central phrase in this promise important for the wording of later promises of obedience is the following: "to whom [Peter] the power to bind and loose was given by the Lord God, and to his aforementioned vicar and his successors to exhibit in all things." This phrase will be contained with minor changes in the promise of obedience for bishops in the Romano-Germanic Pontifical. The concepts of the Petrine power to loose and bind and the present Bishop of Rome as the vicar and successor of Peter were common by the eighth century, and they were seen as very positive elements of society. As the Church became more and more involved in the structures of political power, the concept of Peter and his successors as bishops of Rome having power to make judgments for the ruling of society became important, and with this reality, the power to bind and loose likewise took on more importance. At this time there was no separation of spiritual and temporal power, but we must be careful not to read into these texts our contemporary understanding of Church and state.

Finally, we need to say something about the verb "to exhibit." While it can be translated "to show or display," "to exhibit" is a stronger and more accurate term. This stronger translation is modified by the phrase "in all things," a modifier that will appear and disappear from one text to another as our study continues. What was promised to be exhibited in all things was "fidelity and purity" or "complete fidelity and purity to the holy catholic faith." Here fidelity seems to include the moral aspect of one's purity in following the ways of the faith. In any case, it is personal and demanding of the one making the promise.

In the years 743–44, Boniface attempted a reform of church structure that expected the subordination of bishops to Boniface and the subjection of clergy to diocesan bishops. Included in this structure was the reporting of clergy to their bishops and the charge to examine all itinerant bishops and presbyters before they were to be instituted.[16] This reform basically failed because Boniface was unable to overturn the proprietary church system. However, these structural ideas would be the wave of the future. Boniface was archbishop, with papal authority and pallium at this time. It would seem logical that he would demand from his bishops a promise of obedience similar to that which he made to the Pope. It would likewise seem logical that presbyters would make a promise of obedience to their bishops as vassals would to their lords; that is, placing their hands in the hands of their bishops and promising obedience. In either case, these were actually acts of structural freedom allowing both bishop and priest to work independently from the political powers of the locale. The second structural aspect of such promises was their reciprocal nature. While bishop and priest promised obedience, the person to whom obedience was promised took some responsibility for his subjects—a workable solution for those times.

We find clear evidence of how Boniface views his ecclesial role in some of his correspondence with Pope Zachary (741–52) and Pope Stephen II (752–57). In 742 Boniface writes Zachary in Epistle 49 using language that clearly describes his obedience and devotion to the Church of Rome. He writes that he works under the authority of Peter as a devoted servant and obedient disciple, *under canon law,* and that he will not cease to be obedient to the Apostolic See.[17]

Zachary, in his Epistle 5, writes Boniface about numerous ecclesiastical issues, but he clearly connects Boniface's authority to the pallium. Zachary writes that the use of the pallium demands that one serve the discipline of the Church.[18]

Further, in Epistle 8, to all the bishops and abbots of the Franks,[19] Zachary quotes an interpretation of chapter 9 of the Canons of the Synod of Antioch of 341, which allows for the metropolitan to call

[16] E. Ewig in Jedin, *Handbook of Church History,* 3:13–4.
[17] Migne, *Patrologiae Cursus Completus,* 89:741.
[18] Ibid., 926.
[19] Ibid., 931.

regional synods. While this synod is from another time and place and very Eastern in its ecclesiology, it serves Zachary's purposes well. In any case, Boniface's authority to be metropolitan is clearly supported by the Bishop of Rome.[20] A key phrase in this canon is "according to the ancient law constituted by our fathers," which echoes the "ancient institutions of the holy Fathers" of Boniface's promise of obedience. While serving a new purpose, the traditions of the past were found to be most helpful.

Finally, we mention a letter from Boniface to Pope Stephen. It is Epistle 78, written in 752, and it speaks clearly of how Boniface viewed his service to the bishops of Rome. Here he uses another juridical term, "I pledge" *(spondeo)*, which gives further impetus to the seriousness of Boniface's commitment.[21]

With this documentation we have a clearer understanding of the hierarchial structure favored by both Boniface and Rome in the mid-eighth century. While the authority of the Bishop of Rome was growing, likewise the authority of the local metropolitans was growing. This allowed for a Church that was freer to do what needed to be done.

THE EIGHTH AND NINTH CENTURIES

The political relationship between the kings of the Franks and the power of the Church is the key to understanding this epoch. First of all, they found each other mutually beneficial. The Church needed the king, and later emperor, for its freedom to be Church, and the king found that the Church gave him a unique and anointed position in the realm. Thus we find Boniface anointing Pepin in 751.[22] Likewise, Pope Leo III (795–816) found it to his advantage to anoint Charlemagne on Christmas day in the year 800, and Charlemagne found great comfort in calling himself "king and priest," drawing on themes found in both the Old Testament and the Orient.

Charlemagne took his role fairly seriously. He obtained palliums to honor his metropolitans. While he saw this as honoring his bishops, in fact it put them under the authority of the Pope.[23] From then on, these metropolitans were often seen as papal vicars who acted as intermedi-

---

[20] Mansi, *Sacrorum Conciliorum Nova et Amplissima Collectio*, 2:1323.

[21] Migne, *Patrologiae Cursus Completus*, 89:779.

[22] E. Ewig in Jedin, *Handbook of Church History*, 3:18.

[23] Knowles, *The Christian Centuries*, 72.

aries between the emperor and the episcopate as a whole and who as archbishops confirmed the election of their suffragan bishops.[24]

We still basically have two entities existing side by side, namely, proprietary churches controlled by the lords and diocesan churches controlled by the bishops. With the reforms of Louis the Pious (818–19), we move a step closer to more church control. Some of these reforms included the right of dioceses to elect their own bishops, although the emperor maintained the right to confirm and invest those under his control. Bishops controlled the installation, removal, and conduct of presbyters for proprietary churches. Several important rules were made law. Concerning the presbyterate, the ordination of someone who was not free was forbidden and a legal minimum income was set. This applied to proprietary churches as well as parish churches. Finally, bishops were obliged to ordain those clerics presented to them for proprietary churches once they were examined and found acceptable.[25] Slowly the system of proprietary churches was coming under the authority of the local bishops.

EIGHTH-CENTURY ORDINATION RITES

We have in Ordo XXXIV ordination rites from the early eighth century. These were the basic rites used at Rome with some Gallican influences. The rite for presbyters is very sketchy. The rite for bishops is more involved. We are told that the archbishop enters the church and is seated with the pallium. This is part of the authority of that symbol. Then we have a clear question and statement of purpose, although the language is rather secular.

"And, when they have been led in, they are asked by the Apostolic Lord *(a domno apostolico), What is it, fathers, that wearies (fatigastis) you?* They respond: *Lord, that you would grant us a protector (patronem)."*[26]

The first important concept is that the local clergy request the elect to be made their *patronem.* This seems to confirm the structure discussed above, in which the local church is under the protection of their bishop. The second important concept is the election of the

---

[24] E. Ewig in Jedin, *Handbook of Church History,* 3:166.
[25] Ibid., 109–10.
[26] Andrieu, *Les ordines romani,* 3:608.

bishop by the local clergy. The request comes from the local clergy themselves, and the elect is to be ordained for that local church.

The archbishop then proceeds to interrogate the elect. This *examinatio* is a development of the *examinatio* found in another ancient source, the *Statuta Ecclesiae Antiqua*.[27] The major concern is the moral character of the elect. While there is no promise of obedience, twice he is asked if he has made a commitment or promise *(datio* or *promissio)* that would prevent him from being free, or if he has made any promises against the canons that would determine him to be guilty of simony.[28] The issue here is the freedom of the elect to be a stable bishop for that church.

In Ordo XXXIX we have a late-eighth-century ordination rite for a presbyter. It has heavy Gallican influences. As may be expected, there is no mention of obedience. However, there is the declaration that each presbyter is ordained for a particular place and with a particular title.

"And the pontiff calls with a laud voice each one by his own name to his chair and says: *This presbyter to the third province with this title, that presbyter, etc. (Talis presbiter, regionis tertiae, titulo tale, Ille)."*[29]

There was at this time no need for ritual promises of obedience. The major concern for presbyters and bishops during this first millennium, in terms of obedience, was the need for stability and the freedom to serve the needs of the Church. Stability was seen in terms of presbyters and bishops being ordained for a particular church[30] and in terms of each community having the ministers it needed. Above we mentioned the attempted reforms of Boniface, some of which dealt with itinerant bishops and presbyters and the need for churches to be able to support a presbyter. Freedom to serve had to do with the moral character of the bishop or presbyter and with his fidelity to only the Church and her teachings.

[27] Ibid., 616–9.

[28] Ibid., 608–11.

[29] Andrieu, *Les ordines romani,* 4:283–6.

[30] For an excellent article on the issues of absolute ordination, see Vogel, "Titre d'ordination et lien du presbytre à la communauté locale dans l'Églese ancienne," 70–85.

The last personage, whose colorful life and many epistles make him an invaluable part of any study of this century, is Hincmar.[31] His struggles with both the Bishop of Rome and his own local bishops, including his nephew, give us great insight to how at least this one metropolitan viewed his ecclesial role. The basic issue here is the relationship between the primacy of Peter and the powers of every bishop. Hincmar has no problem with the primacy of the Bishop of Rome, but not at the expense of the authority of the local bishops.

In Epistle 2, addressed to Pope Nicholas I (858–67), he extols the primacy of Peter, especially as seen against the power of the king, but he justifies a bishop's submission to the Pope as part of simple good order.[32] He uses canonical terms such as "holy canons" and "holy laws" as well as feudal terms such as "submissive to" and "subject to" (subditas and subjectos).

Then Hincmar continues by quoting Luke 2:51, Heb 12:17, Phil 2:3, and I Cor 11:16 to give a scriptural basis to his thought. These verses speak of the good order of a family where there is good authority and respect for those in charge rather than the Petrine verses generally quoted to justify papal authority.

In *Epistola* 27 to Pope Hadrian II (867–72) Hincmar states that the power of the keys has been bestowed on all bishops while being careful to accept the unique position of Peter.[33] He reminds Hadrian that nothing is bound or loosed unless it is bound or loosed by blessed Peter.

Concerning the further structure of the metropolitan, in his *Epistola* 30 to his bishops Hincmar uses Canon 6 of Nicaea to justify that not all bishops are equal. The sign of the authority of the metropolitan is the pallium. Again, this is a case of the good order of the Church.[34]

Concerning the relationship between presbyters and bishops, long before getting into the scholastic discussions of whether the episcopacy was one of the orders, Hincmar spoke of both orders as biblically based, one based on the seventy-two disciples sent forth, and

---

[31] We will be following Tavard's excellent article, *Episcopacy and Apostolic Succession According to Hincmar of Reims*, 594–623.

[32] Migne, *Patrologia Cursus Completus*, 126:32–3.

[33] Ibid., 181–3.

[34] Ibid., 191.

one based on apostolic succession. We find this idea in one of Hincmar's letters to his bishops.[35] Here we also find the important idea of presbyters being the second order of priests but sharing in the *sacerdotium* of Christ.

Hincmar goes one step further and states that presbyters also have the Petrine power of the keys in their power to forgive sins. However, bishops control presbyters, again for good order. This is stated in Hincmar's *Schedula* or *Libellus expostulationis,* which he wrote for the Synod of Douzy.[36] Here the power of the keys is part of the power to loose and to bind given to Peter.

Hincmar tried to use his metropolitan position to his advantage between pope and king and between pope and local bishop. While he may have been exceptional because of the magnitude of his personality, his influence was tremendous. Certainly his understanding of the power of the local church is central to any interpretation of the Church in the ninth century. Finally, his view of the presbyterate as an order endowed with the biblical power of the keys is an important link to the development of the presbyterate as the epitome of priesthood that would follow in the scholastic period.

ECCLESIOLOGICAL REFLECTIONS

This period of the Church cannot be understood outside the political context of the development of the Holy Roman Empire or the cultural context of the beginnings of feudalism. In both contexts the major issue is that of order, a good order that would allow all involved the freedom to exist. The order of the political power of Charlemagne and his successors was needed for the Church to survive in the face of the continued immigration of barbaric peoples from the east and Islam from the south. The order of the feudal system was needed to keep society intact. The Church simply became the major player in this development, because it alone could anoint the political powers and give them true authority, and it alone could offer the hope of a better life in the reality of heaven to its members who struggled to scratch out an existence on earth. It is in this context that obedience came to be externalized as a form of giving freedom and security to both Church as institution and its bishops and presbyters

[35] Ibid., 125:1009.
[36] Ibid., 126:609.

as leaders. While this externalization would not be codified in rites until the next century, its reality was lived out in the survival of the institution. In this understanding we can affirm the development of the promise of obedience as the Church striving for the structural freedom to be church, and this is indeed a happy development.

A second reflection concerns the basic issue of the relationship between the Petrine authority of the Bishop of Rome and the apostolic authority of each local bishop. This ongoing tension was simply maintained. It was a matter of each needing the other, a conclusion still valid for our time. A final reflection acknowledges the beginning of the development of the presbyterate as the epitome of priesthood. The relationship of the local presbyter to his bishop is one of the major concerns for any discussion of priesthood today.

2

Ordination Rites and Roman Pontificals

THE ROMANO-GERMANIC PONTIFICAL

As we move into the tenth century the following general observations are helpful. First, a general reading of the times points out that the semblance of order still present in the writings of Hincmar in the previous century was now barely recognizable. In the political scene there were major struggles between the king of the Franks, now more commonly called Germany, and the many and various princes of that kingdom. The common people struggled to scratch out an existence in a society in which they were at the mercy of their feudal lords.

The Church at Rome, while striving to remain independent of all outside political forces, also struggled with the local lords and nobles. What had been Charlemagne's empire was no longer a reality except in the various vassal relationships that certain nobles had with other nobles.

It was at this time that Otto I came to the throne in Germany. He saw his task as the reestablishment of the Carolingian empire. He had himself anointed while seated in Charles's throne by the archbishop of Mainz. He sought to maintain control over the many princes as well as over the nomination of bishops. We must remember that this was an age that did not distinguish between priesthood and kingdom except in function. All were seen as under Christ. The king had been anointed, and he took his responsibility as God's anointed seriously. He gave bishops their investiture, symbolized by the ring and staff, their property, and their secular rights of sovereignty as well as by their ecclesiastical function. In effect, the Church was very much dependent upon the local political powers. However, in the political thinking of the time it was better to be under the king than under the various princes. Finally, Otto I was actually a very religious man who had the best intentions of the Church at heart.[1]

It was also at this time that the great Cluny reform was begun, which, while definitely Gallican in origin, also had a great influence in what we now call Italy. Even more important was the monastic reform, which paralleled Cluny, in the area of Germany then called Lotharingia. This reform was to have great influence on the Romano-Germanic Pontifical. It is helpful to remember that in time of reform the Church almost always turns and returns to monasticism as one central model and source of reform.

This first great pontifical, the one that now carries the name Romano-Germanic, is the fruit of these reforms. We have ample evidence to maintain that it was compiled in Mainz during the reign of Otto I under the direct guidance of William, archbishop of Mainz (954–68) at this time. William was Otto's son and protector of the Abbey of St. Alban.[2] Thus we see William's connection to the reform. The monastic renewal of Lotharingia also had a great influence on Otto and his renewal of the empire, and various monks from Trier formed part of his imperial court. Otto made every effort to support this reform.[3]

This German compilation became a very Roman work in a matter of decades due to the politics of Berengar, who ruled Lombardy as a vassal of Otto, and the spiritual force of Otto's own vision for a new Carolingian empire. Berengar, in violation of his vassalage, had expansionistic tendencies in mind, and in his sights were the territories of the Bishop of Rome. Pope John XII (955–64) asked Otto for help along with offering the imperial crown. Otto came to Rome in 960 where he received the crown and made an oath, one similar to the oath Charles the Fat made in 881, to protect the person of the Pope and the patrimony of Peter.[4]

Otto made many subsequent journeys to Rome. With his deep desire for liturgical renewal in the face of the profound liturgical decadence found in Rome, he simply took this pontifical of Mainz with him to Rome, and it was hungrily devoured in the liturgical vacuum

---

[1] F. Kempf in Jedin, *Handbook of Church History*, 3:201–3.

[2] Vogel, *Medieval Liturgy*, 237.

[3] Kempf in Jedin, *Handbook of Church History*, 3:321–2.

[4] Ibid., 205.

there. In a few short decades it was basically called a Roman book. Thus we have the second stage of that first level of liturgical development; namely, something German now returns to Rome and becomes Roman.[5]

Looking at the text, we see that the ordination rites for presbyters, deacons, and subdeacons is found in one rite in one part of the pontifical entitled "The Order of the Manner in Which in the Roman Church Presbyters, Deacons, or Subdeacons are elected," while the ordination rites for bishops are much more involved, are spread over many rites, and are found in another part of the pontifical. The ordination rites for bishops are not included with the rites for presbyters and deacons because this was the bishop's book for all the ceremonies he could perform. It would be an exceptional ceremony to ordain a bishop for the service of the local church. There was no overriding theological reason to include or not include the ordination rites for bishops with those of presbyters, deacons, and subdeacons.

Second, the ordination rites for presbyters, deacons, and subdeacons make the simple distinction between major and minor orders. Subdiaconate was the first of the major orders. There are no promises of obedience in the rites for the subdiaconate or diaconate. However, in the rite of ordination to the diaconate, in the receiving of the stole we find the following explanation of the stole signifying the candidate's moral character:

"Receive the white stole from the hand of the bishop. Purified from every sordid fault and standing in the sight of the divine majesty, may the conversion of your entire life *(ut omnibus vita* [sic] *tuae conversationis)* offer an example to the people devoted to the name of Christ, and by imitating you, may they acquire a true example."[6]

The significant words here are "the conversion of your entire life," an echo of monastic promises such as those found in the *Rule of Benedict*, which included stability and obedience as well.[7] What is meant here is that the candidate's relationships must be based on the gospel call to purity and right order. Obedience is part of that right ordering

[5] Vogel, *Medieval Liturgy,* 238.
[6] Vogel, *Le Pontifical Romano-Germanique du Dixième Siècle,* 1:27.
[7] Lentini, *S. Benedetto: La Regola,* 522–4.

of relationships. Finally, we need to remember that for every candidate for subdiaconate or diaconate the goal was the presbyterate, and that is where obedience came to be ritualized for the first time within the rite of ordination itself.

Ordination of Presbyters in the Romano-Germanic Pontifical
In the rite for the ordination of presbyters, we find the following structure. After the first reading, the tract, and the litany, the candidate is presented to the bishop. This is followed by an *examinatio*, which flows into a question-and-answer structure, the will you–I will *(vis–volo)* structure, which is a common feature of this and subsequent rites. At the end of this *examinatio* we find the promise of obedience followed by an allocution, which mentions obedience. The promise of obedience takes the following form:

"Will you *(Vis)* be obedient and consenting *(obediens et consentiens)* to your bishop for whose diocese *(ad cuius parrochiam)* you are about to be ordained according to justice and your ministry *(secundum iustitiam et ministerium tuum)?* Resp.: I will *(Volo).*

"May your good and upright will be worthy to bring about a perfection pleasing to God. Resp: And this to God and his holy ones *(hoc Deo et sanctis eius)* who are here present I promise *(promitto)* as I am able to know and strong enough to fulfill. May God and his holy ones help me."[8]

Concerning the structure, we can see that we have an amalgamation of two structures. First we find the *will you–I will* structure followed by the more ancient and personalistic *I promise* structure common to the promises we have already seen. In subsequent ritual development this *promitto* structure will be dropped. Thus, here we find ourselves at a true crossroads of ritual structure.

This development from a personalistic *promitto* to a more formal and juridical *vis–volo* seems to come from the understanding of free consent *(consentiens)*, a concept also central to the issues of marriage at the time. What is included in the concept of *consentiens* is the notion of a pact or agreement.[9] The Church had the responsibility to ask the candi-

[8] Vogel, *Le Pontifical Romano-Germanique*, 30.
[9] Blaise, *Lexicon Latinitatis Medii Aevi*, 236.

date if he willingly and knowingly submitted to the authority of the Church. This was most easily done in the form of a question. Second, while we still have this older and more personalistic form, the structures of ordination rites are moving toward the simpler *vis–volo* form.

The text uses the words "parish" or "diocese" *(parrochia)*. Like "diocese" *(dioecesis)*, "parish" has become part of our common vocabulary. Both terms find their roots in the Greek vocabulary of marriage and running households. In Greek, a πάροχος *(parochos)* was one who goes beside another in a chariot, the ὄχος *(ochos)*, as one who attends a bridegroom. Later he was seen as the administrator of that person's affairs. In Greek, διοίκησιζ *(dioikisis)* is from διοικέω *(dioikeo)*, which means "to manage a house." Both words later came to mean "province" or "district." In our text, it is clear that *parrochia* means what we would today call "diocese." In any case, it is a much larger concept than our modern understanding of parish.

The candidate is being ordained for the diocese of his bishop, which reflects the later development of the proprietary churches. As we saw in chapter 1, one solution was for bishops to take over the proprietary churches and ordain presbyters subject to them. This was a simple transfer of vassalage. Thus the church and its presbyters were free from interference by the local lords. However, this promise of obedience was also concerned with stability. The parish church needed a presbyter. The presbyter needed a church that could afford him a livelihood. This promise gave structural freedom to the local church.

The candidate is asked to be both obedient and consenting. We have already amply discussed the relational aspect of *obediens. Consentiens* adds the important element, mentioned above, of a commitment freely and willingly given. Again, this is part of the need at that time to elicit a free response on the part of the candidate.

Finally, the question states that this promise is made according to justice and the ministry of the candidate. "Justice" seems to indicate that the promise is made in accord with the plan of God. "Ministry" seems to indicate the function of the service to be done. The candidate is called to service. Thus both the call and the promise are relational in nature.

The bishop continues and prays that the candidate's good and upright will may be worthy to bring about a perfection pleasing to God. The divine initiative of grace is acknowledged. Again we see the desire for the will to be free and correctly followed.

Then the text turns to the older *promitto* structure. It is influenced by the form of the monastic promises found in the *Rule of Benedict* and is used in many monasteries. The "this to God and his holy ones" *(hoc Deo et sanctis eius)* echoes the "before God and his holy ones" *(coram Deo et Sanctis eius)* of the *Rule of Benedict* (58.18).[10] We need to remember that this form contains a commitment to God and the Church. As in early monastic promises, there is no mention of the person to whom the promise is made, as this is a later development.

Second, there is an emphasis on the personal limitations of the person who promises these things as he is able to know and strong enough to fulfill them. This is a promise made by a finite human being and made out of his humanity. Finally, God and his holy ones are called upon for help.

We have seen that for some centuries and in many places a bishop would elicit from those being ordained to the presbyterate a ritual promise of obedience. The issue is that this important but extrinsic ritual became part of the rite of ordination. It is true that the content of a promise of obedience is indeed kindred to the content of the *examinatio.* It has to do with the character and intentionality of the candidate, and as in our modern rites of ordination, it made ritual sense to include such a promise there. However, we must remember that in the next two ritual developments, this promise was placed after Communion. It seems that this promise of obedience was moved here as a matter of expediency, since this was the only time the bishop would be present to elicit such a promise from the candidate.

Now we come to the allocution. Its opening directions are "Then he speaks to the people in the following words." It is basically a summation of what has happened. In this allocution we find this statement: "This is necessary because it is easier for him who is ordained to show obedience to the one to whom he had promised obedience in ordination."[11] Here again we find affirmed the rationale for placing the promise of obedience here in this public rite of ordination. In the context of consulting the people about the suitability of the candidate, we are told it is easier for the one ordained to show obedience to the bishop to whom he promised obedience at his ordination as a public commitment.

[10] Lentini, *S. Benedetto*, 524.
[11] Vogel, *Le Pontifical Romano-Germanique*, 30.

Ordination of Bishops in the Romano-Germanic Pontifical

In the midst of the various things a bishop can bless, we find the instructions and rites for the ordination of bishops. It begins with a decree on the election of a bishop by the local clergy and people, under the title "Here begins the examination for the ordination of a bishop according to the Gauls."[12] Then we are told that the elect is to be examined according to the Carthaginian canon, which is actually the text of the *examinatio* of the *Statuta Ecclesiae Antiqua*,[13] although here it is accredited as coming from the Fourth African Council. Finally we arrive at the rite of ordination itself.

The rite begins with its own *examinatio*. This repeating of the *examinatio* is a development to keep in mind in subsequent rites. Here we seem to have the normal conservative desire in textual compilation to keep an older form of the *examinatio* along with the newer forms in the rite itself that serve their purposes better. In our text we have numerous questions concerning the moral character and faith of the elect. The structural context is that of the *vis–volo* form now common. The third and fourth questions contain the content of the promise of obedience:

"Will you exhibit in all things fidelity and subservience *(fidem et subiectionem)* to blessed Peter, to whom the power to bind and loose was given by God, and to his vicar and his successors? R: I will.

"Will you exhibit fidelity and subservience *(fidem et subiectionem)* to the holy church of Mainz (Mogontiensi), and fidelity and subservience *(fidem et subiectionem)* to me and my successors? R: I will."[14]

The first part is almost word for word from the promise of obedience of Boniface.[15] The major addition is "fidelity" and "subservience," which were already part of the vocabulary of obedience present in the correspondence of Boniface. While these are feudal

---

[12] Ibid., 200–1.

[13] This text is given as an introduction to the rite of ordination of bishops in Vogel, ibid., 196–7. The original can also be found in Andrieu, *Les Ordines Romani*, 3:616–9.

[14] Ibid., 202.

[15] ". . . cui a Domino Deo potestas ligandi solvendique data est, et praedicto vicario tuo atque successoribus eius, per omnia exhibere," Migne, *Patrologiae Cursus Completus*, 89:803–4.

terms, they reflect the reality of how the Church maintained its freedom to function in this society. *Fidem* here is a personal term expressing one's desire to know and follow the wishes of the Pope. Thus "fidelity" is a better English translation than "faith" because of its relational image. *Subiectionem* here is a structural term expressing obedience to the Pope. "Subservience" is perhaps a better English translation than a notion of subjection. Being subservient to the Pope allowed the local bishop the freedom to work. It was neither understood nor experienced in any way as limiting the bishop's power. Also, at this time in their history the Germanic people had a special love for the successor of Peter, almost a sort of Peter cult, especially centered around the Petrine power of binding and loosing. Pilgrims went to Rome as part of their penance for sins to receive forgiveness there.[16] This public promise reflected the piety and faith of that age.

The second part is a clear structural reference to the obedience owed the archbishop by a suffragan bishop. Here the elect is asked to pledge fidelity and subservience[17] to the archbishop of Mainz (Mogontiensus, or later, Moguntinus) and his successors. This is one clear reference to the origin of this text and a clear description of the ecclesial structure of the time. In subsequent centuries this relationship will develop into one where the archbishop has a diminished role, and this will be reflected in the rite. Finally, we note that obedience is owed first of all to the local archdiocese. This naming of the local church before the mention of the local bishop reflects a proper order of ecclesiological realities; namely, the bishop is called to the service of a local church. This entire ritual with the same *examinatio* with its promise of obedience is repeated, with the many explanatory rites proper to an episcopal ordination, under the title "The manner by which a bishop in the Roman Church is ordained."[18] This reflects the ongoing stage of its compilation and acceptance in Rome as a Roman book.

Structurally, as in the rite of ordination for presbyters, the promise of obedience is part of the rite itself as part of the *examinatio*. As in the rite of ordination for presbyters, the rationale seems to have been that

---

[16] Kempf, in Jedin, *Handbook of Church History*, 3:292.

[17] *Subjecto* carries with it the sense of being a vassal. See Blaise, *Lexicon Latinitatis Medii Aevi*, 874.

[18] Vogel, *Le Pontifical Romano-Germanique*, 205–26.

the ritual questioning of obedience made sense as part of the questioning of the moral character and faith of the elect.

The promise of obedience is much older than this first ritual expression, as chapter 1 has shown. It is not intrinsically tied to the rite of ordination. The Tridentine reform will place it as part of an *examinatio* to be done prior to ordination. However, at this time, it obviously was advantageous to have it here, celebrated in such a public forum.

Finally, we must balance the rather simplistic hierarchical structure envisioned by the rite with the reality of the Church at that time. Papal jurisdiction over the local church was not accepted without question. We have, for example, the synodal decisions of Verzy in 991, which placed the local churches up against papal authority.[19] Likewise, the relationship between archbishop and suffragan bishops continued to be, as today, dependent on the personalities involved. Yet this pontifical put forth, in the minds of its compilers, the best of a vision of a Church unified under God and king.[20]

The Romano-Germanic Pontifical: Ecclesiological Reflections

First, we simply accent the development of this first great pontifical and its influence on the history of the Church. It was a book that served the needs of its time and had a far greater influence than its compilers ever dreamed of. It is worth reflecting on what role liturgical books play in the furthering of the faith in our time. How can our liturgical books foster the prayer and prayer language of the people who pray them? How can a local people take a liturgical book and make it their own? More specific to our study, how are changes and additions in the promises of obedience, which carry a particular rationale intended by its compilers, prayed by the ministers and people of the local community? Can we shape our notions of obedience by their ritual form? This last question is very important for the recent revisions of ordination rites.

Second, the most significant question in the development of the Romano-Germanic Pontifical is the adding of an important but extrinsic promise of obedience to the rite of ordination itself. Is this the best place for such a promise? Obviously, later compilers of ordination rites felt free to move it. We must keep this question in mind as we study the revisions of our day.

[19] Kempf, in Jedin, *Handbook of Church History*, 3:297–8.
[20] Vogel, *Medieval Liturgy*, 235–7.

Third, by the time of this pontifical, we are already losing the personalistic *promitto* form that formally and informally served the Church up until then. Its replacement by the more juridical *vis–volo* form seems to be a loss of the richness of an earlier age.

Fourth, in the rite of ordination of bishops the role of the archbishop, the metropolitan, is accented. This is part of our ancient tradition and still part of the Eastern tradition, whereby the election and ordination of bishops is much more under the guidance of the local metropolitans. Perhaps this tradition is worthy of further reflection for our time.

ORDINES ROMANI OF THE TENTH CENTURY

Ordo XXXV is an early-tenth-century text and reflects earlier rites. There are no promises of obedience in the ordination rites. Ordo XXXV A is a transitional text with some influences from the Romano-Germanic Pontifical, but there are no promises of obedience. Ordo XXXV B is a late-tenth-century text, and here we find the full influence of the Romano-Germanic Pontifical.[21] The text is titled "In the name of Christ, here begins the order for the calling and examining or consecrating one elected bishop." Thus we are dealing with the rite of ordination for bishops. In the *examinatio* we find the following text:

"Will you exhibit fidelity and subservience to blessed Peter, to whom the power to bind and loose was given by God, and to his vicar and his successors? Resp: I will.

"Will you exhibit fidelity and subservience to the holy church of Iuvavum (Iuvavensi), to me and my successors? Resp: I will."[22]

It is almost word-for-word the text from the Romano-Germanic Pontifical except that "to exhibit in all things" is reduced to simply "to exhibit." The text for obedience to the local archbishop is a faithful copy of a text of Ordo XXXV B from Salzburg, reflecting that Iuvavensus, or Iuvavum, is an ancient diocese in the Noricum Ripense near Salzburg.[23] Obviously, the name of the diocese would change from place to place.

[21] Ibid, 176–7. The texts are in Andrieu, *Ordines Romani*, 4:32–110.
[22] Andrieu, *Ordines Romani*, 4:102.
[23] Ibid., 84.

First, we need to acknowledge two great personages, Pope Gregory VII and Gracian.

Pope Gregory VII (1073–85) signaled a new understanding of papal authority. While his famous confrontation with Henry IV in 1077 at the castle of Canossa has been immortalized in history, his pontificate and the Gregorian Reform marks the beginning of a Roman initiative that in some sense has never ceased. This is especially true in terms of liturgical books.

The so-called *Dictatus Papae* (Sayings of the popes) of Gregory VII contains in concise form the relationship between Pope and bishop envisioned by Gregory. Here are the statements that are of interest:

"3. That the Roman pontiff alone can depose or re-establish bishops.

"4. That his legate, even if of inferior rank, is above all bishops in council; and he can give sentence of deposition against them.

"7. That it is permitted to him alone to establish new laws for the necessity of the time, to make new peoples into congregations, to make an abbacy of canonical establishment and vice versa, to divide a rich bishopric and combine poor ones.

"13. That it is permitted to him to transfer bishops, under pressure of necessity, from one see to another.

"14. That throughout the church, wherever he wishes, he can ordain a cleric.

"25. That he can depose and re-establish bishops without a meeting of the synod."[24]

While these statements never became law in Gregory's day, they foretell the direction of papal-episcopal relationships. Especially telling is the concept of the universal jurisdiction of the pope.[25] Yet the overriding pastoral concern is that of necessity. As always, the needs of the Church were central.

As we move into the twelfth century, as a prelude to Gracian, we find a subtle but important development during the time of Pope

---

[24] Caspar, *Das Register Gregors VII*, 202–8. English translation in Osborne, *Priesthood: A History of the Ordained Ministry in the Roman Catholic Church*, 210–1.

[25] Y. Congar, "Les ministères d'Église dans le monde féodal jusqu'à la réforme Grégorienne," 83.

Paschal II (1099–1118) concerning the relationship between the Pope and all bishops, in particular metropolitans. There was no desire to bind all bishops to Rome. The metropolitans were seen as representing papal authority in their areas. But these same metropolitans were now required to go to Rome in person to receive the pallium and take an oath of obedience to the pope, which included for the first time the obligation of periodic visits to the threshold of the apostles.[26] This obligation would, in a later time, be asked of all bishops.

While the reception of the pallium and the power to oversee the election and perform the ordination of suffragan bishops seemed to enhance the authority of metropolitans, a second and ongoing development helped further the actual diminishment of their power. Using the False Decretals of Pseudo-Isidore compiled in the ninth century, suffragan bishops could and did appeal directly to the pope when in conflict with their metropolitans. This is the background for the slow breakdown of the metropolitan system of election and ordination of bishops, which, while still ritually present in these centuries, would disappear by Trent.

Finally, the First Lateran Council (1123) in its decrees shows much regard for the rights of local diocesan bishops in their sacramental ministry.[27] For example, in the context of the relationship between the local bishop and the monks living in his diocese, we find a clear teaching for monks to be obedient to the local bishop and a clear preference for only those monks ordained by the hands of the local bishop to be responsible for sacramental ministry.[28] This understanding of the power of each local bishop would further diminish the authority of metropolitans in the West.

With the Decretals of Gracian (ca. 1140) we have the first great codification of church law. Gracian took all the canons then known and considered authentic, including some later discovered to be false such as those of Pseudo-Isidore, and made them accessible to the church leaders of his time and subsequent ages. Part of this codification included the above movement of the enhancement of papal authority to the diminishment of episcopal authority and the right of any bishop to appeal directly to the pope.[29] The importance of Gracian's Decretals

---

[26] Kempf, in Jedin, *Handbook of Church History,* 3:430.

[27] Ibid, 429.

[28] First Lateran Council, 16, Tanner, *Decrees of the Ecumenical Councils,* 1:193.

[29] F. Kempf, in Jedin, *Handbook of Church History,* 3:426–45.

are that these became the source of both ecclesial action and study for centuries to come.

With this historical understanding in mind, we turn to the Roman Pontificals of the twelfth century. They are called pontificals in the plural because the surviving copies are so divergent that there could not have been a common Roman archetype. This means that there was no single, official version of the Romano-Germanic Pontifical in use in Rome at this time. Yet these divergent texts form enough of a family of manuscripts that they can be studied in themselves, separate from the Romano-Germanic Pontifical.[30]

In the chapter entitled "The order for the manner in which in the Roman Church deacons and presbyters are elected," we find no promises of obedience for the rite of ordination for presbyters. What this seems to indicate is that any promise of obedience was done at some time other than the rite of ordination.

In the chapter entitled "Here begins the order for the calling and examining or consecrating one elected as bishop according to the custom of the Roman Church," in the *examinatio* of that rite, we find the following promise of obedience:

"Will you exhibit in all things fidelity and subservience to blessed Peter, to whom the power to bind and loose was given by God, and to me, his unworthy vicar and my successors? Resp: I will."[31]

What we find here is an amalgamation of the double promise found in both the Romano-Germanic Pontifical and in the *Ordines* of the tenth century. Obviously, part of that movement is the fact that the pope and the metropolitan of the elect in this rite is one and the same. But this also, both theologically and ritually, reflects the movement toward the enhancement of papal authority. It is also curious that "in all things" returns. The major theological loss in this amalgamation is that there is no mention of the Church, local or universal. The earlier texts were more specific in their ecclesiology. Here the Church of Rome is simply implied in the mention of Peter.

Finally, this family of manuscripts contains a profession made by archbishops to the pope. It is a development of the promise of obedience

<hr>

[30] Vogel, *Medieval Liturgy,* 249–50.
[31] Andrieu, *Le Pontifical Romain au Moyen-Âge,* 1:142.

made by Boniface and contains the important and above-mentioned promise for the *ad limina* visit.[32] There is a strong personal commitment asked of the archbishop to the pope. Seen in the context of this feudal age, this strong personal commitment can easily be understood. However, there is very little concern about doctrinal or moral purity. This perhaps clearly demonstrates one problem with the structural placement of a promise of obedience in the context of the *examinatio* of an ordination rite. The *examinatio* is concerned with doctrinal and moral purity, a context in which obedience does not seem to fit easily.

THE PONTIFICAL OF THE ROMAN CURIA OF THE THIRTEENTH CENTURY

The manuscripts for the pontifical of this period form a more coherent family than the group of manuscripts for the pontificals of the previous century. There is the use of the singular and the supposition of a common archetype. There are grounds to claim that it must have been the result of the leadership of the masters of ceremonies of the Lateran. Yet there are three editions, with slight variations, that existed side by side. The third of these editions accompanied the popes to Avignon and competed with the work of William Durandus, our next personage.[33]

In the chapter entitled "The order of the manner in which in the Roman Church deacons and presbyters are elected" we do not find a promise of obedience. What we do find is the beginning of a postcommunion rite, which will be further developed in subsequent pontificals.[34]

"After the pontiff has received communion, but before the pouring (of the Precious Blood), those who were ordained, after they make a confession and kiss the right hand of the pontiff *(facta confessione et osculata dextera pontificis),* let them receive holy communion from the hand of the pontiff, and then receive the kiss of peace from him as well as from the presbyters and deacons. Then let them receive the (Precious) Blood from the hand of the deacon who sang the gospel. Then they return to their place around the altar."[35]

[32] Ibid., 290–1.

[33] Vogel, *Medieval Liturgy*, 252.

[34] Aubry, "A propos de la signification du <<Promitto>>," 1063; Kleinheyer, *Die Priesterweihe im Römischen Ritus*, 214.

[35] Andrieu, *Le Pontifical Romain*, 2:350.

The important words here are "after they make a confession and kiss the right hand of the pontiff," as these will form an essential part of the postcommunion of subsequent rites of ordination for presbyters. By "confession" here is simply meant a personal acknowledgment of one's unworthiness and also one's belief in the Real Presence, perhaps without words. In William Durandus we will find the recitation of the Creed. In the Tridentine reform we will find a rather curious recitation of the *Confiteor*. By the kissing of the right hand of the pope we have a ritual act of veneration of the hand of the bishop, which holds sacred things, in this particular circumstance Holy Communion. Both subsequent rituals will have the promise of obedience at this point.

Perhaps this directive is part of a post-Berengar development in eucharistic theology. One is asked to profess belief in the Real Presence. More likely it is part of the development of the understanding that the presbyter was the one who could confect the sacrament of the Eucharist. What is curious is that the ritual expression of that power is found earlier in the rite of ordination with the words "Receive the power to offer sacrifice to God and celebrate mass for both the living and the dead in the name of the Lord."[36]

Perhaps we can understand this directive as a ritual repetition of the kiss of submission at the end of the rite of ordination itself. The rite of ordination occurs just before the reading of the gospel. Here is that directive:

"After this blessing and ordination are completed, those who were ordained presbyters by the Lord Pope, having first kissed the feet of the pontiff *(osculatis primum pedibus pontificis)*, give the kiss of peace to the pontiff, then to the cardinal bishops, priests and deacons, and then to the rest of the prelates and ministers who are around the altar."[37]

This rite is rich with the papal tradition of using the kissing of the feet as an act of submission.[38] In the thirteenth century it seems that there was reason to repeat some act of submission and profession at the time of Communion, and that is the rite we find there. This seems to be supported by the repetition of the reception of the kiss of peace from the pope at Communion time.

[36] Ibid., 348.
[37] Ibid., 349.
[38] Ibid., 357, 364, 367, 374.

One final point is how these rites separate the reception of the Body and Blood of the Lord. The "after making a confession and kissing the right hand of the pontiff" occurs before the reception of the Body of Christ, followed by the kiss of peace. Then the presbyter receives the Blood of Christ from the hands of the deacon. In subsequent rites the promise of obedience will take place after reception of both species. We are in a period of ritual flux, and thus it would be common to repeat ritual elements rather than simplify them. This seems to be the rationale for this postcommunion directive.

In the chapter entitled "Here begins the Order for the calling or examining or consecrating of one elected bishop when he was elected by the Roman Church but not first questioned by the Roman Church," we find the ordination rite for bishops. The title suggests that this *examinatio* has a multipurpose nature and is dependent on circumstances. Here we find the same promise of obedience for bishops that we saw in the rites from the twelfth century. What is added is a version for when someone other than the pope ordains:

"Will you exhibit in all things fidelity and subservience to blessed Peter, to whom the power to bind and loose was given by God, and to his vicar, our most holy *(sanctissimo)* Father, Lord N., the most high Pontiff and his successors? Resp: I will."[39]

With the use of *sanctissimo* we have an indication of the increased attention given the person of the Bishop of Rome. Again we note the theological loss of the mention of the local church. It would seem that here was given an opportunity for a bishop other than the pope to remind the elect that he was being ordained bishop for a local church.

THE PONTIFICAL OF WILLIAM DURANDUS

At the very end of the thirteenth century (ca. 1293–95) William Durandus, bishop of Mende in the south of France, compiled a pontifical in three books. William never intended his work to be a universal pontifical, but its clarity of arrangement and quality of substance, along with the fact that it prescribed all the episcopal functions for bishops in Latin Christendom, caused it to be very popular and useful.[40]

[39] Ibid., 356.
[40] Vogel, *Medieval Liturgy,* 253–5.

However, William was well prepared both to do such a task and to have it well received. Earlier in his career he was brought to Rome as the vicar general to Martin IV (1281–85), the most French of the thirteenth-century popes. William was also one of the great canonists of his time.[41] He had ample experience with the Pontifical of the Roman Curia and was well known by church leaders throughout Europe.

Nevertheless, the greatest single reason for the influence of the Pontifical of William Durandus was the papal schism of the late fourteenth century with the development of the Avignon papacy. Here the work of William became far more important than the pontificals the popes had brought with them from Rome. When they returned to Rome in the pontificate of Martin V (1417–31) it was this pontifical that returned with them. Thus we have in a nutshell the second level of liturgical development in both its stages; namely, something Roman goes to Avignon and then something French returns to Rome.

Ordination of Presbyters in the Pontifical of William Durandus

In the Pontifical of William Durandus we find all the rites of ordination in order, beginning with the minor orders and concluding with the rites for bishop. This reflects a more consistent arrangement of rites than to have those for bishop in a separate place.

In the chapter entitled "The ordination of presbyters" we find directives allowing for the rite of ordination to occur at two possible places, one before the reading of the gospel and one after the reading of the gospel but before the Creed.[42] The directive about the Creed will be important to keep in mind as we study this rite.

In the rite we find that the many and varied questions that had made up the *examinatio* are reduced to one. Then the bishop reads the allocution we saw earlier in the Romano-Germanic Pontifical. Since this allocution was basically a summation of the *examinatio*, it covers the same issues, including the statement we studied concerning obedience.[43] Of course, the problem here is that we no longer have the promise of obedience in this place. Obedience is implied here and will be ritualized after Communion. The second curious note is that this allocution is declared to be part of the statutes of the Council of

---

[41] H. Wolter in Jedin, *Handbook of Church History,* 4:236.
[42] Andrieu, *Le Pontifical Romain,* 3:364.
[43] Ibid., 365.

Carthage. This is an echo of the then-believed source of the *Statuta Ecclesiae Antiqua*.

As to why the *examinatio* was shortened or why the promise of obedience was moved, it would seem that it was shortened because of the development of doing such questioning at another time.[44] In particular we will see this in the ordination rite for bishops. There was no need to repeat. Accordingly, the promise of obedience was moved because the structure of the *examinatio* no longer supported such a promise.

Now we turn to the postcommunion rite, for it is here that we find the promise of obedience.[45] After the newly ordained presbyter receives Communion in both species from the hands of the bishop, and after the singing of the communion antiphon, we find the recitation of the Creed, which the earlier directive had placed after the rite of ordination.[46] Then the bishop lays hands a second time on the head of the ordinand and prays "Receive the holy spirit, those whose sins you forgive are forgiven, those whom you retain are retained." Actually, the imposition during the rite of ordination involved only one hand.

The next directive is a rubric to roll down the chasuble and to say these words concerning the stole: "The Lord clothes you with the stole of innocence." This is part of the vesting rite of the newly ordained presbyter in the Romano-Germanic Pontifical. However, in the vesting rite of the Pontifical of William Durandus this small verse is left out and we find it here. The stole is a common symbol for the power of ministry. Thus it would seem that we have a development of a rite to meet a new need.

That new need seems to flow out of the thirteenth-century understanding of a presbyter as one who has the power to confect the Eucharist and forgive sins. This development must be understood in light of the scholastic thinking about orders.[47] The major scholastic theological tenet that concerns our study is the teaching that the full power of orders rests in the order of presbyters.[48] The episcopacy was

[44] Brandolini, "L'evoluzione storica dei riti delle ordinazione," 84–5.

[45] Andrieu, *Le Pontifical Romain*, 3:371–2; Kleinheyer, *Die Priesterwiehe im Römischen Ritus*, 204–16.

[46] Brandolini, "L'evoluzione storica dei riti delle ordinazione," 86.

[47] Osborne, *Priesthood*, 204–12; Ryan, "Legacy of the Schoolmen," 3–38.

[48] There is even documentation for the power of priests to ordain, especially minor orders. See Y. Congar, "Faits, problèmes et reflexions à propos du pouvoir

not considered an order. Since the presbyterate also now included the power of the keys, the power of forgiveness of sins, this had to be ritually expressed.

The ordination rite already expressed the power of the presbyter to confect the Eucharist in the words "Receive the power to offer sacrifice to God and celebrate masses for both the living and the dead." The question is not so much why the second ritual expression for the forgiveness of sins was added but why it was added postcommunion and with a second laying on of hands.

The first reason for such a development seems to flow out of the biblical and theological understanding of the reception of the Holy Spirit being intrinsically connected with the power of forgiveness of sins. With this understanding came the ritual gesture of the laying on of hands. The question of the relationship of this laying on of hands with the gesture of the laying on of hands in the ordination rite was not as significant in their eyes as perhaps in our eyes, because for them the issues of the matter and form of the sacrament of orders were still open.[49] The laying on of hands had to do simply with the ritual giving of the power of the Holy Spirit to forgive sins.

Second, as we saw in the ordination rites for presbyters in the Pontifical of the Roman Curia of the thirteenth century, there were the beginnings of a postcommunion rite that included both a profession of faith and an act of veneration, and it was here that William chose to add the various elements yet to be celebrated.[50] He placed the Creed here. This was simply the only place left to add this laying on of hands with the reception of the power to forgive sins.

We finally come to the promise of obedience. The entire directive states:

"Then a second time each candidate goes to the bishop, placing his hands between the hands of the bishop (*ponens manus suas iunctas inter manus episcopi*) who says: Do you promise me and my successors obedience and respect (*Promittis michi et successoribus meis obedientiam*

---

d'ordre et des rapports entre le presbytérat et l'épiscopat," 107–28; Beyer, "Nature et Position du Sacerdoce," 356–73; Ryan, "Episcopal Consecration: Trent to Vatican II," 133–50.

[49] Nichols, *Holy Orders,* 129. Osborne, *Priesthood,* 300–1.

[50] Brandolini, "L'evoluzione storica dei riti delle ordinazione," 85.

et reverentiam)? And he responds: I promise *(Promitto)*. This is done if the candidate is not subject to another bishop *(Et hoc nisi alteri sit subiectus)*. Then, still holding the candidate's hands in his hands the pontiff kisses him saying: The peace of the Lord be with you always. And he responds: Amen."[51]

This is the first time the ritual of the joining of hands *(immixtio manuum)* is part of the rite of ordination. While certainly this ritual action was a common part of the feudal rite of vassalage and its use was one of the solutions to the issue of proprietary churches, it is a late development in the actual rite of ordination. It seems that this addition of the *immixtio manuum* is an influence from the rites of religious profession.[52]

We have lost the *vis-volo* structure and have returned to at least the use of the word *promitto*.[53] For the first time in the rite of ordination for presbyters we find the mention of the successors of the bishop, and there is no mention of parish as in the Romano-Germanic Pontifical. This is clearly part of a theological development from a presbyterate connected to a local church or parish to a presbyterate connected to the local episcopacy, at least in terms of jurisdiction. The earlier issues of proprietary churches are finally dead. The powers of the local bishop are finally and ritually absolute, again in terms of jurisdiction.

This promise is made to the person of the bishop, *michi*, and thus is very personal. The words "obedient and consenting," which we saw in the Romano-Germanic Pontifical, have been replaced with "obedience and respect" *(obedientiam et reverentiam)*. The emphasis has moved from the intentionality and free will of the candidate to his personal connection to his bishop.[54] *Reverentiam* refers to one's personal relationship to the bishop, so "respect" is perhaps an accurate translation. Perhaps this too reflects the theological reality of a school of thought that viewed the presbyter as the one with the fullness of orders and its corresponding emphasis on the bishop as the one who could give the jurisdiction to act on those powers.

[51] Andrieu, *Le Pontifical Romain*, 3:372.

[52] Kleinheyer, *Die Priesterwiehe im Römischen Ritus*, 215.

[53] Aubry, "A propos de la signification du 'Promitto,'" 1067.

[54] *Reverentia* has the sense of the inclining of the head of one who is under the jurisdiction of another, Blaise, *Lexican Latinitatis Medii Aevi*, 797.

Then this promise of obedience is clarified, stating that a presbyter can only promise obedience to the ordaining bishop if he is not subject to another bishop. Again this is part of the issue of jurisdiction.[55] Finally, this whole ritual is closed with a rite of peace, just as the post-communion ritual in the Pontifical of the Roman Curia of the thirteenth century.[56]

This promise of obedience was placed here because the placement of the promise of obedience in the *examinatio* of the rite of ordination for presbyters was not seen as primary. It never became part of the rites in Rome. That, plus the ritual diminishment of the *examinatio*, forced William to find a new place. Second, the beginnings of a ritual development after Communion in the Pontifical of the Roman Curia of the thirteenth century was ripe for the placement of such a rite. Finally, this seems to be a compromise between the German and Roman traditions.[57] William Durandus felt it was important to ritualize this promise of obedience. Its form and placement were of lesser significance.

Nevertheless, there are some theological issues that were not fully understood at the time. If the promise of obedience is done before ordination, it is seen as a condition for orders. If it is done here, post factum, it can only be seen, at best, as a seal of an implied obedient relationship between presbyter and bishop.[58] Thus we see the rationale for the movement of this promise in the reforms of the Second Vatican Council. This points to two important theological issues. The first is the extrinsic nature of the promise of obedience in relation to the rite of ordination. The second is that now the promise of obedience is in a diminished ritual role.

The promise of obedience of presbyter to bishop had lost its historical importance. No longer were proprietary churches an issue. The high age of feudalism had passed. As we saw in the rite, the act of vassalage had to be described. By the thirteenth century the need for presbyters to make a promise of subjection to their bishops was of lesser importance than the freedom of the Church.

This seems to be confirmed by the teachings of the Fourth Lateran Council (1215). This council used the term "obedience" only once in

---

[55] Aubry, "A propos de la signification du 'Promitto,'" 1063.

[56] Kleinheyer, *Die Priesterweihe im Römischen Ritus*, 214.

[57] Ibid., 213–4.

[58] Brandolini, "L'evoluzione storica dei riti delle ordinazione," 86.

the context of priesthood, and this is the context when there are different rites in the same diocese. Here the presbyters of those other rites
are asked to be obedient and subject to the local bishop in all things.[59]
Concerning the issue of oaths of fealty made to laymen, the Fourth
Lateran Council prohibited such oaths.[60] The council did not give a rationale for the issue but simply stated that such oaths were contrary
to the divine right of clerics in the Church. This implies that the historical issues had changed and there was no longer any need for the
Church to concern itself with acts of vassalage. However, ritually this
act of vassalage and its promise of obedience continued, although
now in a diminished postcommunion rite.

Ordination of Bishops in the Pontifical of William Durandus

This chapter is entitled "The examination, ordination and consecration of a bishop," which shows the transitional stage of the terminology for bishops. "Consecration" became the word used in subsequent
rites. The *examinatio* is expected to take place the Saturday evening
before the actual consecration.

The next day, or Sunday, the rite begins with the same *examinatio*
we saw in the Romano-Germanic Pontifical. This points to a ritual
crossroads where there are two traditions such that later development
will choose one over the other. Here, for example, the Tridentine reform will keep only the first and much longer *examinatio*. We also
need to remember the strong teaching of the Fourth Lateran Council
(1215) on the importance of the local bishop diligently examining the
one elected to a bishopric and the penalty of doing it improperly.[61] Finally, here we have the beginnings of an *examinatio* done at a time
other than the rite of ordination.

Returning to our text, in this *examinatio* we are given a promise of
obedience in the form now familiar to us:

"Will you exhibit fidelity, subservience and obedience according to
canonical authority *(fidem, subiectionem et obedientiam secundum canonicam auctoritatem)* to blessed Peter the apostle to whom the power to
bind and loose was given by God, and to his vicars the roman pon-

---

[59] Fourth Lateran Council, 9, Tanner, *Decrees of the Ecumenical Councils,* 1:239.
[60] Fourth Lateran Council, 43, Ibid., 253.
[61] Fourth Lateran Council, 26, Ibid., 247.

tiffs, to the holy church of Bituricae (Bituricensi) and to me, its minister, and to my successors?"[62]

We finally have a good amalgamation of the two promises found in the Romano-Germanic Pontifical; namely, of obedience to the pope and obedience to the local church. The vicars of Peter are placed in the plural to include all his successors. Then the local church is mentioned; in our text it is the archdiocese of Bituricae in Gallia Aquitania. What is more important, the local bishop calls himself the minister of that church. Finally we have an expansion of the promise of fidelity and subservience to include "obedience according to canonical authority." This is a juridical concept of obedience, one based on observance of laws rather than personal relationships. This formula will remain in the Tridentine reform. However, the change to a more juridical understanding of obedience based less on the historical context of vassalage and more on the notion of jurisdiction for ministry in the Church is not without serious implications.

At the end of Mass, after the final blessing, we have the promise of obedience of the newly consecrated bishop. The directive states that this is the same *professio* made by the metropolitan after the examination and just before the consecration. This promise is read, being held above the altar and the Book of the Gospels.[63]

While much of this promise is a development of the promise found in the Roman Pontificals of the twelfth century,[64] the most significant changes are the additions of an "I promise" section and the use of the term "being obedient." With the mention of the written promise in relation to the altar, we seem to have an influence from monastic promises. Finally, we must note the strong metropolitan structure still present in this promise.

The Pontifical of William Durandus: Ecclesiological Reflections

We can note three different but related ritual moments that are dealt with in transition in the Pontifical of William Durandus and that are still issues for our day. Obviously, the first ritual moment is the actual promise of obedience itself. While essential in the good order of

[62] Andrieu, *Le Pontifical Romain*, 3:379.
[63] Ibid., 392.
[64] Andrieu, *Le Pontifical Romain*, 1:290–1.

things although not intrinsic to the rite of ordination, when do we ritually celebrate it? If during the rite of ordination, then when in that rite? The Church has felt free to move it and try different ritual arrangements. Finally, by this time the promise of obedience had lost its original context and had become more juridical. Thus the question of when to ritualize a promise of obedience is still open.

The second ritual moment is the *examinatio.* Ritually it is much older than the promise of obedience and of a much broader scope, as it deals with moral character and doctrinal purity. Again, we have an essential element for the good order of things. The question is again when and where to ritualize it. It certainly has a role in the public celebration of orders, as it ritualizes the intentionality of the candidate. However, the question concerns the ritualizing of a much longer and involved process, which by the time of the celebration of the sacrament is implied by the rite itself. Much of the history of the promise of obedience depends on the history of this larger ritual. We must continue to ask if this is the best place for a promise of obedience.

The third ritual moment is, finally, the ordination. By the time we arrive at this moment, what elements have already been ritualized and no longer need to be part of this final celebration? Here we have the issue of ritual repetition. More importantly, are we trying to reaffirm certain doctrinal elements by ritually repeating them?

We continue to struggle for a fuller understanding of ecclesiology. In particular, the grounding of the ordination of either presbyters or bishops in the service of a particular local or universal Church is often diminished in favor of a more personal commitment to the person of the pope or bishop. While such personal commitment is essential again to good order, the more essential element of ministry to the people who make up the Church must not be omitted.

Finally, the major underlying theological issues in the development of the Pontifical of William Durandus are those of the relationship between bishop and presbyter and, in particular, the theology of the presbyterate as the fullness of priestly powers with its corresponding theology of the power of jurisdiction of the bishop. While this whole theology has been inverted by the thinking of the Second Vatican Council, the issues, both theological and ritual, have yet to be thought through. This is part of the work yet to be done.

Any study of the Council of Trent and its reform must be prefaced by a deep appreciation of both the tremendous challenge of the times and the great work it was able to accomplish. Suffice it to say that the Council of Trent was able to preserve what was considered the best of the tradition of the Church at the time while at the same time leaving undecided those issues it was unable to resolve. This methodological overview is essential if we are to understand what Trent taught and what it left open for subsequent councils.

We begin with session 6, during which the decree on justification was voted on and passed by the council Fathers, on January 13, 1547. This decree also contains a short decree on the residence of bishops and others of lower rank.[65] The issue here is the abuse of certain bishops who, by their absences, were not giving good ministry. Put simply, the Roman pontiff can take action against such bishops and provide bishops for those churches. What is important is the continuance of the metropolitan structure in carrying out such an action, such that metropolitans were to be responsible for an absent suffragan and the oldest suffragan for an absent metropolitan. This structure is still an important part of our Western tradition.

Session 7 dealt with sacraments in general and on March 3, 1547, passed the first decree on the sacraments. Also passed at this time was a second decree on ecclesiastical reform, which dealt with some issues of orders. Number 13 demands that all those to be ordained, both bishops and presbyters, must submit to an examination by the local ordinaries.[66] Here we have simply reemphasized the need for such an examination, but it is extrinsic to the rite of ordination.

The main session to deal with the sacrament of orders was session 23, which on July 15, 1563, passed the basic teachings of Trent on this sacrament. The basic doctrinal context is that of the eucharistic sacrifice and the power to forgive sins. The presbyter was ordained to celebrate the eucharistic sacrifice and to forgive sins. Orders was one of the seven sacraments. In the sacrament of orders, a character is imprinted that cannot be deleted or removed. Bishops are part of this hierarchical order, and they are higher than presbyters because they can confirm and ordain. However, bishops do celebrate the Eucharist, and

---

[65] Tanner, *Decrees of the Ecumenical Councils,* 2:681–3.
[66] Ibid., 689.

certainly they have the power of the keys. The election to ordination does not depend on the authority of the people or any secular power. However, the fathers at Trent did not resolve the issue of the relationship between bishop and presbyter.[67] This is one very clear example of the methodology of the Council of Trent. It stated what it could be sure of and left the rest in its traditional form. Here is the significant portion of the text:

"The holy council further declares that, apart from the other ranks in the church, bishops in particular belong to this hierarchical order and (as the same apostle says) have been made by the holy Spirit *rulers of the church of God;* and that they are higher than priests *(presbyteris)* and are able to confer the sacrament of confirmation, to ordain the ministers of the church and to fulfill many other functions, whereas those of lower order have no power to perform any of these acts."[68]

What was resolved by the Fathers at Trent is that the episcopacy is part of the sacrament of orders and that bishops are successors in place of the apostles. Their main charism is that of guiding the Church in ministry, a very biblical image. Finally, bishops are the ones to confirm and ordain. No longer is there any confusion on the power of the episcopacy.

Session 23 continues with its decree on reform, whereas Canon 7 deals with the examination of one to be ordained presbyter. What is significant is that the bishop is to summon all involved to the city on the Wednesday before the ordination, or when he chooses. There, with the help of presbyters and other wise men, there is to be a "thorough examination and enquiry into the family, personality, age, education, conduct, doctrine and faith of the ordinands."[69] Clearly we have the structure for an examination done prior to the rite of ordination. In fact, this structure of dates, using the Wednesday before the ordination, is due to the use of the ceremonial structure of ember days for ordinations four times a year, at the changing of the seasons. What is missing is a direct mention of the promise of obedience. In fact, there is no mention of such a promise of obedience in the entire text of the teachings of the Council of Trent on orders.

[67] Osborne, *Priesthood*, 252–63.
[68] Tanner, *Decrees of the Ecumenical Councils*, 2:743.
[69] Ibid., 747.

Further, we must separate the vow of obedience taken by religious from both the ritual promise of obedience in ordination rites and the living out of that important reality in the life of the Church. Having made these distinctions, we can simply say that in the teachings of the Council of Trent obedience was not seen as an issue separate from the good order of things implied in both the teachings on priesthood and in the areas covered in the examination. It was seen as a spiritual virtue, one to be lived out in the presbyterate. It had lost its original context. It was taken for granted that one would be obedient to his bishop, the bishop who ordained him, and the ritual celebration of such a promise in the postcommunion of the rite of ordination would suffice for its ritual realization.

Finally, we come to session 24, which on November 11, 1563, passed the Tridentine teachings on marriage. Also at this time was passed a decree on reform, which included in Canon 1 the basic plan for the election of bishops still in use today.[70] After calling for prayer and the desire to choose the best person to be shepherd of the people, the council makes a disclaimer in that it wishes not to change any arrangements operative at the present time. While part of this was due to the uncertainty of the politics of the time, it is consistent with the methodology of the council to leave unresolved issues in their traditional form.

Then the council calls for the traditional provincial or metropolitan synod to draw up a formula of examination, which is to be approved by the Roman pontiff. Included in this public dossier is all the personal information and the profession of faith of the person under consideration for bishop. This is sent to the Roman pontiff, who, with the various cardinals of the Roman Curia, makes a decision.

Important here is the profession of faith, since it will be this profession of faith that will have the greatest influence on the promise of obedience for bishops.

We now turn to those reforms. The first important development that concerns us is the election of Pope Pius V (1566–72), who in a few short years set the Tridentine reform on a solid path. Most important to him were the election of bishops who would support the reform and the formation of seminaries that would prepare priests in that same spirit.[71]

[70] Ibid., 759–61.
[71] Jedin in Jedin, *Handbook of Church History*, 5:499–503.

More important, in a secret consistory held on April 18, 1567, Pius V declared that every Italian bishop must be examined in Rome by a commission he set up. On May 3 of the same year those who were archbishops were charged with examining those under consideration for bishop and abbot. This new structure eventually led to the founding of the Congregation of Bishops in 1588 under Pope Sixtus V.[72] Thus we see the development of the structure called for in the council. Finally, Pius V took monasticism as his model of reform. Monastic obedience is one key to understanding the developments of Tridentine reform. Using a strong hierarchical model, Pius V saw fidelity to the council as measured by obedience to Rome.[73]

Our next personage is Pope Gregory XIII (1572–85), who was most important for transforming and expanding papal nunciatures into instruments of church reform and a form of ecclesiastical government.[74] It would be this structure that would foster the expansion of papal control of the process of election of bishops, a structure familiar today.

Our final personage is Pope Clement VIII (1592–1605). While it was he who authored the Tridentine Pontifical, he furthered papal control over the examination of bishops for Italy and for those of royal nomination. The major concerns of these examinations were the qualities of the person under consideration for bishop, especially the age-old concern about residency and the new concern for fidelity to the reforms of Trent. This became the major work of the Congregation of Bishops.[75]

Finally, we can express this final level of liturgical development, namely, the movement from Rome to the entire Latin Church. Since Trent there has been a serious attempt to unify and centralize things liturgical in the Roman Rite. For the most part this has been successful. Only since the Second Vatican Council has there been any attempt at the second stage of this level, the struggle of the inculturation of the Roman Rite in the many cultures where it is celebrated. This is work yet to be done.

The Pontificale Romanum *of 1596: The Ordination of Presbyters*

The structure of this pontifical follows that of William Durandus, beginning with the minor orders and ascending to the diaconate,

[72] Pastor, *History of the Popes,* 17:220.
[73] Jedin and Alberigo, *Il Typo Ideale di Vescovo secundo la Riforma Cattolica,* 183–4.
[74] Jedin in Jedin, *Handbook of Church History,* 5:504.
[75] Pastor, *History of the Popes,* 24:189–90.

presbyterate, and episcopacy. The rite of ordination for presbyters is entitled "The Ordination of a Presbyter." The directives call for the ordination to take place after the first reading and the tract but before the gospel. The candidate is presented, and the examination is a simple question of worthiness. This is followed by the same allocution from the Romano-Germanic Pontifical that was present in the Pontifical of William Durandus, with the same issues of the mention of obedience without the promise having been made in the ritual at this place. Thus far, we have a basic copy of William Durandus. Then follows the rite of ordination with the laying on of hands and the normal explanatory rites. This is followed by a concelebrated Mass, one of the two times such was allowed, the other being the Chrism Mass on Holy Thursday.

Then we come to the postcommunion. After the bishop has received Communion, we find this curious directive.[76] If there were any deacons or subdeacons ordained in the same ceremony, they come up and show reverence. The bishop himself reverences the Eucharist on the altar *(Pontifex facta reverentia Sacramento),* and then the deacons and subdeacons say in a low voice the *Confiteor.* The bishop then gives an absolution. However, the directive says that the presbyters are not to say the *Confiteor* nor are they given the absolution, because they have concelebrated with the bishop. In fact, if there were no other orders, deacons and subdeacons, ordained, this rite is omitted. Then the presbyters are given Communion. This seems to be the final development of the "after making a confession," which we studied in the Pontifical of the Roman Curia of the thirteenth century. The rest is a basic copy of William Durandus. After having received Communion, the communion antiphon is sung, *Iam non dicam* (I no longer call you servants). Then the Creed is recited. The second laying on of hands with the giving of the Spirit for the forgiveness of sins is made. This is followed by the promise of obedience. Here we are given several options for the various situations that could arise. He places his hands in the hands of the pontiff, who says, if he is the ordinary:

"Do you promise me and my successors respect and obedience? *(Promittis mihi, et successoribus meis reverentiam, et obedientiam?)* I promise. *(Promitto.)"*

[76] *Pontificale Romanum,* 57.

If he is not the ordinary, he says to the secular presbyter *(Presbyteris saecularibus):*

"Do you promise your ordinary *(Pontifici Ordinario)* respect and obedience?"

Or if he is a religious *(Regularibus):*

"Do you promise your superior *(Praelato Ordinario)* respect and obedience?"[77]

Here *praelatus (Praelato Ordinario)* refers to the superior of an exempt order or an abbot *nullius* of a monastery, while *pontifex (Pontifici Ordinario)* refers to the local bishop.[78] The issue is that of jurisdiction, not priestly power. Thus the major theological concern now bound up with this promise of obedience is that of priestly faculties.[79] To be a presbyter in good standing, a presbyter who could offer Mass and hear confessions, implied a presbyter who was obedient to his bishop or superior. As we discussed earlier, the original context for this promise of obedience had changed. It was now seen in a juridical context, one in which a newly ordained presbyter promised obedience to his bishop or superior in return for the faculties to function as a presbyter.

The Pontificale Romanum *of 1596: The Consecration of Bishops*

The title "The Consecration of One Elected as Bishop" tells us much about the ongoing development of the episcopacy as an order. While the Council of Trent did teach that the episcopacy was part of the sacrament of orders, it did not resolve how this was to be understood. The issue was not that bishops had the power of jurisdiction. Rather, the issue was how or where a bishop received his power of jurisdiction. Did a bishop receive his power by divine right by virtue of his ordination and as a successor of the apostles, or did a bishop receive this power of jurisdiction from the pope? How was one to understand his bond with a local, particular church and his bond with the univer-

---

[77] Ibid., 57–8.

[78] Catalanus, *Pontificale Romanum,* 1:261–3.

[79] For a recent study of the juridical aspects of obedience see Schneider, "Obedience to the Bishop by the Diocesan Priest in the 1983 Code of Canon Law," 19–29.

sal Church in terms of episcopal powers?[80] The theological relationship under question here is that of the local bishop to the pope, a relationship that still needs further study. What our title displays is a compromise. While maintaining episcopacy as an order, the use of the word "consecration" keeps both the issues and the various traditions alive to be resolved at some later date.

The opening directive refers to the importance of the new system of examination. It states that no one can be consecrated unless he has been examined, either by an apostolic letter if he lives outside the Curia or in person, even in the presence of the pope.[81]

When all is ready, the consecration begins with the following dialogue:

"Most Reverend Father, holy mother Church asks that you raise (*sublevetis*) this Presbyter, here present, to the responsibility of the episcopacy (*ad onus Episcopalus*)."[82]

This is the same wording as the Pontifical of William Durandus. The verb here conveniently avoids the issue of ordination or consecration. However, instead of the familiar question of worthiness, we next have the question of whether there is an apostolic mandate. This is new and reflects the desire for papal approval of all new bishops. This mandate is then read. The major reason for dropping the question of worthiness is that the issue has already been answered in the new structure of examining those under consideration for bishop.

Then we have the option for an oath of fidelity. At this point, politically we are in a state of flux, and only those bishops in the Papal States and in countries that had such relationships with Rome would make such an oath. In fact, it is the same oath that archbishops take when they receive the pallium. Finally, it is a further development of the promises we have studied, which include obedience to the pope and the *ad limina* visit. What is significant is that it is called an oath.[83] We have here a much more juridical understanding of obedience.

---

[80] See Alberigo, *Lo sviluppo della dottrina sui poteri nella Chiesa universale: Momenti essenziali tra il XVI e XIX secolo;* Jedin, "Zur Theologie der Episkopates von Trindentinum bis zum Vaticanum I," 176–81; Ryan, "Episcopal Consecration: Trent to Vatican II," 135–40.

[81] *Pontificale Romanum*, 60.

[82] Ibid., 61.

[83] Ibid., 61–3.

The first line is almost the same as the promise of obedience taken by archbishops to the pope, which we studied from the pontificals of the twelfth century.[84] The major addition is the term "being obedient." What is curious is that the use of *promitto* from the Pontifical of William Durandus is lacking.[85] Likewise, there is no mention of a written promise in relation to the altar nor any sense of the metropolitan structure of the Church. The whole promise is expanded, and the development of the *ad limina* visit reflects the reporting of pastoral ministry to the pope, which still today is quite extensive. This wording and the subsequent reality places the question of the relationship between bishops and pope in a very practical light. We continue to struggle to harmonize this demand with the tradition that each bishop is a successor of the apostles.

Then we come to the *Examen*. While similar to previous examinations, the elect responds to the beginning of the process: "Thus with my whole heart I wish to consent and to obey in all things,"[86] which is an echo of previous promises of obedience. The third question of the *Interrogation* contains the promise of obedience, one very similar to that found in William Durandus:

"Will you exhibit in all things fidelity, subservience and obedience according to canonical authority *(fidem, subjectionem, et obedientiam secundum canonicam auctoritatem)* to the blessed Apostle Peter, to whom the power to bind and loose was given by God, to his Vicar our Lord, Pope N., and to his successors, the Roman Pontiffs? R. I will."[87]

The major development here is the greater emphasis on the person of the present pope. The Pontifical of William Durandus, by its more general and impersonal use of the plural form of vicar, as we discussed earlier, gave a broader ecclesial sense to the position of the vicar of Peter. Here, with the return to the use of the singular for vicar, obedience to the present pope is strengthened.

The rest of the *Interrogation* is mainly concerned with credal statements. However, the major issue is the relationship between the profession of faith, previously given and sent to the pope, and this ritual

[84] Andrieu, *Le Pontifical Romain*, 1:290–1.
[85] Ibid, 3:392.
[86] *Pontificale Romanum*, 64.
[87] Ibid., 64–5.

expression.[88] What we need to remember is that this rite intended to cover all possible situations. What was intended on most occasions of episcopal consecrations is that the examination and profession of faith would have been done earlier. It would only be done here, before the Mass for the rite of consecration, when necessary. This maintains the tradition of the promise of obedience for bishops to the pope as extrinsic to the rite of ordination or consecration.

Then the Eucharist begins and proceeds up until the gospel, followed by the rite of consecration for bishops. The gospel is read after the giving of the books of the gospels, and Mass continues from there. After Communion we have a series of further rites and blessings pertaining to the episcopacy.

Thus the promise of obedience for bishops is part of the *Examen* before Mass and before the rite of ordination. While seen as very important, it was extrinsic to the rites of consecration.

The Pontificale Romanum *of 1596: Ecclesiological Reflections*

First of all, we have in both the teachings of the Council of Trent and the ritual reform of the pontifical, especially in the case of the rite of ordination for presbyters, a much more juridical understanding of the promise of obedience. In fact, this promise of obedience for presbyters is now bound up with the corresponding giving of faculties to perform one's presbyteral powers. Obedience implies that a presbyter will do what his bishop wishes in return for the jurisdiction to do his presbyteral work. A disobedient presbyter will have his faculties withdrawn. Thus obedience for presbyters had become a method of both good order and control. While in earlier times obedience was a source of structural freedom to do presbyteral work, it had now become the major method by which a bishop controlled those presbyters who worked in his diocese. We had lost the structurally freeing role that the promise of obedience had played in earlier times. Yet any study of the canonical history of irremovable pastors and exempt orders will show how we had struggled to keep some sense of the relational aspect of obedience. The question for our time is whether a ritual promise of obedience can create the good order of church ministry envisioned by the compilers of our rites.

---

[88] Nabuco, *Pontificalis Romani*, 256–9.

Second, with the development of a stronger papal tradition in terms of both the election and the *ad limina* visits of bishops, we have basically lost the metropolitan structure in our Western tradition. Moreover, the relationship between local bishop and pope is one that struggles to find fuller balance. While teaching that bishops are truly the successors of the apostles, there has been a strong development to make bishops almost mere legates to the pope. This tension is evident in the teachings of both the First Vatican Council and the Second Vatican Council, which we will study. This important relationship has not been adequately resolved.

Finally, if the promise of obedience takes on a much more juridical understanding, what effect does this have on the even more important living out of that Christian virtue? This struggle is also seen in the history of monastic and religious life, and to this area we now turn in order to obtain a fuller understanding of obedience in the life of ministry in the Church.

3

Monastic and Mendicant Rites

The rationale for such a chapter is obvious. First, the vocabulary and ritual actions of monastic and mendicant rites of profession and the blessings of abbots, which include obedience, and the promises of obedience in ordination rites, have a reciprocal relationship such that the developments in the ritualization of the promise of obedience in monasteries and orders will influence such promises in ordination rites and vice versa.

Second, the relationship between bishops and abbots, presbyters and monks, bishops and orders, diocesan presbyters and mendicants, as reflected in the ritualization of obedience and the historical working out of these relationships, had and still has an influence on the development of the promise of obedience in ordination rites.

Finally, since the Church often turns and returns to monasticism and religious life as ideals worthy of emulation by its ministers, a basic study of how obedience has been ritualized in monastic life and religious life is helpful.

THE *RULE OF BENEDICT*

Even though a historical study of monasticism is far more complicated, because of the singular influence of Benedict on Western monasticism we can begin with the *Rule of Benedict*.[1] Specifically, we are concerned with chapter 58 of the *Rule of Benedict*, which in descriptive form gives us a very simple ritual that is still the basis of all monastic professions.

---

[1] de Vogüé, "La Règle de Saint Benoît," 181:29–79. Pulickal, "A Study of the Rite of Religious Profession and Its Adaptation to the Cultural Traditions of India," 1–15.

"Now this shall be the manner of his reception. In the oratory, in the presence of all, he shall promise his stability, the conversion of his life and obedience; and this before God and his Saints *(coram omnibus promittat de stabilitate sua et conversatione morum suorum et oboedientiam coram deo et sanctis eius)*, so that he may know that should he ever do otherwise he will be condemned by him whom he mocks. He shall embody this promise of his in a petition, drawn up in the names of the Saints whose relics are there and of the abbot who is present. *(De qua promissione sua faciat petitionem ad nomen sanctorum, quorum reliquae ibi sunt, et abbatis presentis.)* Let him write this document with his own hand; or if he cannot write, let another do it at his request, and let the novice put his mark to it and place it on the altar with his own hand. *(Quam petitionem manu sua scribat aut certe, si non scit literas, alter ab eo rogatus scribat; et ille novitius signum faciat et manu sua eam super altare ponat.)*

"When he has placed it there, let the novice himself at once intone this verse: *Receive me, Lord, according to your word, that I may live: do not let me be confused by my expectation.* Let the whole community repeat this after him three times, adding at the end of all the *Gloria Patri.* Then let the novice prostrate himself before the feet of each monk, asking them to pray for him; and from that day let him be counted as one of the community. If he possess any property, let him either give it before-hand to the poor, or make a formal donation bestowing it on the monastery. Let him keep back nothing at all for himself, as knowing that thenceforward he will not have the disposition even of his own body. So let him, there and then in the oratory, be stripped of his own clothes which he is wearing and dressed in the clothes of the monastery. But let those clothes, which have been taken off him, be put aside in the clothes-room and kept there. Then, should he ever listen to the persuasions of the devil and decide to leave the monastery, let them take off him the clothes of the monastery and so dismiss him. But his petition, which the abbot took from off the altar, shall not be returned to him, but shall be preserved in the monastery."[2]

Ritually, we are dealing with a promise, the *promissio*, which is writ-ten down and called a petition, the *petitio*, and then placed on the altar. Then we have a prostration followed by the changing into the habit.

[2] Lentini, *S. Benedetto*, 520–33; Hanslik, "Benedicti Regula," 136–7.

This *promissio* is a single promise consisting of three elements: his stability, the conversion of his life, and obedience. "Stability" simply refers to the desire to remain in the monastery. *Conversatio morum suorum* has a more difficult history. It literally means a change in the relationships of one's life habits, his *mores*. In many subsequent texts it will be changed to *conversio morum*.[3] The issue was the difficulty of understanding the deeper meanings of *conversatio* as a relational term, one that implied a commitment to right relationships in one's life based on how one spoke and listened to the Lord and others. *Conversio*, or a simple turning or conversion, made easier sense. "Obedience" is listed as the third element without any further qualifications except that it is made before God and his saints, along with the other two elements. Thus this promise is made before God and before his saints, who now are witnesses to it.[4] There is no mention of observing the Rule, a point that will be central to subsequent texts.

Then we have a movement from an oral promise to a written petition made in the name of the saints whose relics are there and in the name of the abbot who is present. We are not told what is in the written petition. If the monk is illiterate, someone else writes it for him, but he puts his mark on it. This petition is then placed on the altar.

The written petition was, first of all, personal.[5] It certainly would include aspects of the three elements of the promise, but not in any determined form. While it is written in the presence of the abbot and there is no mention of a personal commitment to him, obedience to the abbot is implied by the observance of the entirety of the Rule.[6] The

---

[3] de Vogüé, "La Règle de Saint Benoît," 186:1324–9; Pulickal, "Study of the Rite of Religious Profession and its Adaptation to the Cultural Traditions of India," 17–8; Yeo, *Structure and Content of Monastic Profession,* 161–2, Mohrmann, "La langue de Saint Benoit," 341–5; Lentini, *S. Benedetto,* 522–3.

[4] Pulickal, "Study of the Rite of Religious Profession," 19; Yeo, *Structure and Content of Monastic Profession,* 131.

[5] Pulickal, "Study of the Rite of Religious Profession," 21; Yeo, *Structure and Content of Monastic Profession,* 132.

[6] Two passages from chapter 5 of the *Rule of Benedict* help to clarify that obedience to the abbot or other superiors is implicit in the promise of obedience made here. ". . . Mox aliquid imperatum a mairore fuerit, ac si divinitus imperetur, moram pati nesciant in facendo. . . . Ut non suo arbitrio viventes, vel desideriis suis et voluptatibus oboedientes, sed amulantes alieno iudicio et imperio, in coenobiis degentes, abbatem sibi praeesse desiderant." Lentini, *S. Benedetto,* 114–8.

petition is placed on the altar. We must be careful not to read into this text more than is there. We do not have as yet a ritualized formula for the promise, much less a vow.[7] What we have is a very simple rite for the commitment of a monk to life in the monastery.

Second, because there are three elements in the promise, we must keep these elements in relationship to one another. There is only one promise. Thus obedience must be seen in its relationship to stability and conversion of one's way of life.

Third, we must see the written petition as the most important aspect of this ritual, because it was the written petition that would be the personal commitment of the monk and would contain the actual promise. It was the petition placed on the altar that was the sign of the reality of this new relationship.

EARLY COMMENTARIES ON THE *RULE OF BENEDICT*

To flesh out what might have been the wording of such a promise, we turn to the early commentaries on the *Rule of Benedict*.[8] Our first commentary is that of Smaragdus, from the early ninth century, which contains the following:

"I promise in this monastery my stability and the conversion of my life and obedience according to the rule of Saint Benedict before God and his holy ones *(Ego . . . promitto stabilitatem meam et conversationem morum meorum et oboedientiam secundum regulam sancti Benedicti coram Deo et sanctis eius)*."[9]

Here we have the description of the formulary written in first-person form. The addition of "according to the rule of Saint Benedict" is a most important change. The promise is to observe the three elements according to the Rule. While Smaragdus allows for a rather in-

---

See also Böckman, "RB5: Benedict's Chapter on Obedience," 109–30 for an excellent study of chapter 5 and its issues for today.

[7] Yeo, *Structure and Content of Monastic Profession*, 23.

[8] Here we will follow Yeo, *Structure and Content*, 139–66.

[9] Ibid., 143. The text is from Smaragdus, "Expositio in Regulam S. Benedicti," *Corpus Consuetudinum Monasticarum* 8, ed. A. Spannagel, Siegburg: P. Engelbert (1974) 295.

volved petition, his commentary implies that the above wording is to be part of the written petition.[10]

Our next commentary is that of Hildemar, which is likewise from the ninth century but perhaps a generation later than Smaragdus. His promise is as follows:

"I promise my stability and the conversion of my life and obedience before God and his holy ones *(Promitto me de stabilitate mea et conversione morum meorum et obedientia coram Deo et sanctis eius)."*[11]

Here we have a strange Latin construction, especially the addition of *me* and the return to the ablative case with *de* as found written in the Rule. This may be part of the general decline in the comprehension of Latin and can perhaps be supported by the further change of *conversatione* to *conversione*. The former term didn't make sense anymore from the point of view of a literal translation.[12]

More important to our study is Hildemar's understanding of obedience. Using a type of *via negativa,* stating what obedience is not, he seems more concerned with humility than submission:

"Obedience is not about having prosperity or adversity. It is not to unwillingly seek honor or pleasure or the prosperity of this age but to willingly seek the sadness, reproach and adversity of this age."[13]

Finally, Hildemar tells us very little about the petition except that it is to be placed on the altar according to the Rule.

Next we come to Pseudo-Paul, who seems to date from around the same time. The version of the promise found there confirms some of the problems in understanding the Latin in the original text that we touched on above:

"I promise my stability and the conversion of my life from this age and obedience before God and his holy ones *(Promitto de stabilitate mea*

[10] Ibid., 144.

[11] Ibid., 148. The text is from Hildemar, "Expositio Regulae," *Vita et Regula Ss. P. Benedicti una cum Expositione Regulae,* ed. R. Mittermüller, Regensburg (1880) 539.

[12] Ibid., 161–2, where Hildemar understood *conversatio* as concerned with people's places of dwelling and their lives. Thus, *conversio* made easier sense.

[13] Ibid., 163. The text is from Mittermüller, *Vita et Regula Ss.P. Benedicti una cum Expositione Regulae,* 541.

et conversione morum meorum saecularium et oboedientia coram Deo et sanctis eius)."[14]

The strange use of *me* is not in the text. Again we find *conversione* instead of *conversatione*. However, to show their difficulty with the concept of *conversatione morum suorum,* we find the addition of "from this age," as if to remind the monk what he was converting from.

Finally we come to a text, perhaps used by Benedict of Aniane, from the early ninth century:[15]

"I promise my stability and the conversion of my life and obedience according to the rule of S. Benedict before God and his angels *(Ego ille promitto de stabilitate mea et conversione morum meorum et oboedientia secundum regulam S. Benedicti coram Deo et angelis eius)."*

The text returns to a simpler rendition of the Rule, but more important is the influence that Benedict of Aniane would have on later Benedictine rituals.[16] Concerning the petition, we read only that something is to be written during the actual rite, at least a signature, as opposed to something written beforehand.

In summation, the first significant issue for our study is the importance of something being written down. It is this written petition that is the symbol of the promise and that is placed on the altar. At this time the content is rather fluid.

The second important issue is that the promise is to live according to the *Rule of Benedict,* and this implies living under the authority of the abbot. There is no sense of the vassal relationship first copied in the promises of obedience of presbyters to their bishops. This promise is concerned with monastic life as a whole, of which obedience is only a part. Stability had the importance of first place among the three elements, and obedience was seen as part of the day-to-day living out of the Christian life.

---

[14] Ibid., 150. The text is from Paulus Warnefridus, "Expositio," *In Sanctam Regulam Commentarium ad XIV saeculorum ss. Benedicti nativitatis annum,* Monte Cassino (1880) 443.

[15] Ibid., 151. The text is from Mittermüller, *Vita et Regula,* 546. The use of *et angelis eius* is not unanimous.

[16] Kempf in Jedin, *Handbook of Church History,* 3:320.

Finally, we note the placing of the petition on the altar. It is this element that will undergo the greatest change with the coming of the mendicants. However, the concept of a promise in writing and its ritual connection to the altar will become part of the rituals for both abbots and bishops.

THE ROMANO-GERMANIC PONTIFICAL

In the Romano-Germanic Pontifical the order of rites concerning monastic life begins with the consecration of virgins and then continues with abbesses and abbots before arriving at the rites for monks. The rationale for this ordering of rites seems to be one of usage by the local bishop. In general, there would be more houses of consecrated women than monasteries of men, and the local bishop would be more concerned with abbots than with monks, since normally the local abbot would receive monastic promises. Finally, these rites would concern those monasteries under direct control of the local bishop and those abbot-bishoprics still in existence.[17]

Here we find two rites that deal with monks and promises. The first is entitled "The Order for becoming a monk." What is most curious is that there is no mention of a written petition being placed on the altar. The heavy emphasis concerns the putting on of the new habit.

Even more curious is the omission of a prayer concerning obedience, considering that there are two other prayers, one that deals with stability and one that deals with conversion. A reading of these prayers seems to indicate that obedience is somehow incorporated in the monastic concept of stability for the monk, as we read that the monk "promising his stability in this monastery submits to the yoke of your law."[18]

There is a strong presence of the concept of promise in these two prayers with the use of the terms *promittendo, promissa, promisit, promissionis,* and *promittere. Conversum* is used, indicating the change we saw in the commentaries on the *Rule of Benedict,* but there is no mention of the habits of life *(mores)* to be changed. Finally, we have the beginnings of using baptismal images connected to conversion with the presence of the words "to work on purifying his heart and pour forth grace upon him."

[17] Ibid., 273–6.
[18] Vogel, *Le Pontifical Romano-Germanique,* 71–2.

The second rite is entitled "The Ordination of a monk."[19] What we find here is a description of a preparation rite for monastic profession that includes the veiling of the head for seven days and a curious analogy of profession as a second baptism.[20] There are three prayers, the second and third of which mention obedience but in the much broader context of a holy and humble life. Also in this third prayer we find for the first time the use of the term "vow" *(votum)*.[21] This seems to be an influence from the prayers for the consecration of virgins, which speak eloquently of their vow and all the nuptial images that word invokes.[22]

Concerning the abbot, we find one rite, "The Ordination of an abbot," or blessing of an abbot, that is helpful to our study. The opening allocution speaks of the examination of the abbot to ascertain "if he wishes to observe his purpose *(propositum)* and the rule of Saint Benedict, and diligently instruct those subject to him that they might do the same."[23]

The term "purpose" *(propositum)* was already in use in the Veronense Sacramentary for masses "For holy virgins."[24] This term conveys the idea of betrothal or a spousal relationship.[25] It is repeatedly found in the Romano-Germanic Pontifical in the prayers for the consecration of virgins.[26] Thus we have an enrichment of the abbot's relationship to his monks but in the nuptial images of consecrated life.

More important is the examination of the abbot to see if he wishes to observe the Rule. There is no mention of the word "obedience," either to the Rule or to any local bishop or archbishop. We are still in a state of fluidity in the usage of terms to express the reality of one's commitment to the rule of a monastic way of life.

In summation, we must emphasize the importance of obedience according to the Rule, which would imply submission to an abbot or

---

[19] For the imprecision of terms like "ordo" and "ordinatio," see P. Rouillard, "Ministères et ordination en occident," 108–11.

[20] This covering of the head and its baptismal image is first mentioned in the commentary of Hildemar, Yeo, *Structure and Content,* 149, text in Mittermüller, *Vita et Regula,* 539.

[21] Vogel, *Le Pontifical Romano-Germanique,* 72–4.

[22] Ibid., 42–3.

[23] Ibid., 62.

[24] Mohlberg, *Sacramentarium Veronense,* 138.

[25] Pulickal, "Study of the Rite of Religious Profession," 28.

[26] Vogel, *Le Pontifical Romano-Germanique,* 40–4.

bishop without explicitly mentioning it. However, this reality is expressed in numerous ways, often in other contexts and often without the use of the word "obedience." Second, the use of a written petition is completely lacking. It seems that by the tenth century, at least in those monasteries governed by this pontifical, we have moved completely into the tradition of oral promises. Third, the idea of obedience is understood as part of monastic life and thus is a much different concept than that developed among the secular clergy of the same time. Fourth, in its monastic context obedience took on nuptial and baptismal images. In particular, it seems that some of the images of a consecrated life of virginity influenced the development of ritual prayers for monastic life, at least as envisioned in the Romano-Germanic Pontifical. Finally, and most importantly, there was a certain freedom to shape these rites according to the perceived needs of the time. As in our particular study of ordination rites, we find here developments in monastic rites that are both dependent on previous rites and open to new historical realities.

THE ROMAN PONTIFICALS OF THE TWELFTH CENTURY

In the Roman pontificals of the twelfth century, in the central texts we find rites for the consecration of virgins, abbots, and abbesses, and one rite, "The Order for becoming a monk," for monks. None of these mentions promises or obedience. In the appendix we find this rite, "Here begins the order for becoming a monk," and it is here we find significant texts. After an opening exhortation we find the basic elements of the monastic promise in a *vis–volo examinatio* form:

"Therefore, sons, leaving this age you have fled to God. Standing before Him and before this holy altar *(coram eo et coram hoc sacrosancto altari)*, and before the brothers who are present here, with your own mouth say if you wish to renounce this age and its pomp. They respond: We do wish.

"Do you wish to assume the conversion of your lives *(conversionem morum vestrorum)* and leave and renounce the affection of your parents? Resp.: We do wish.

"Do you wish to profess obedience according to the rule of Saint Benedict *(profiteri obedientiam secundum regulam sancti Benedicti)*, renouncing even your own will? Resp.: We do wish.

"The abbot says: May the Lord help you.

"Then those assisting at the altar, in the presence of the abbot and the entire congregation, read their professions *(professiones)* as the rule prescribes:

"I brother N., deacon or presbyter, promise my stability and the conversion of my life and obedience according to the rule of saint Benedict *(promitto stabilitatem meam et conversionem morum meorum et obedientiam secundum regulam sancti Benedicti)* in this venerable monastery of Casino in the presence of the Lord abbot N.

"That which has been read *(Quam perlectam)* is placed upon the altar."[27]

First, we notice that "before God and his holy ones" has become "before Him and this holy altar." Since there is no mention of relics, unless they are implied by the ones in the altar, we no longer have the mention of the saints as witnesses. The presence of the brothers is now far more important. Second, "conversion" is understood in a negative sense, the leaving of family affection. Third, obedience is to the Rule, but again it is seen in terms of humility or the renunciation of one's own will. It is curious that stability is not included in these questions.

Then we have an oral profession, actually a reading of a promise like the ones we have seen, but in a better Latin construction, using the accusative form for the three elements. This promise, which has been read, is then placed on the altar. Thus we have returned to the petition being placed on the altar. However, there is no mention of anything being signed.

THE PONTIFICAL OF THE ROMAN CURIA OF THE THIRTEENTH CENTURY

In this pontifical we have an "Order for becoming a monk," but it is a listing of the prayers found under the same title in the pontificals of the twelfth century, and there is no mention of promise or obedience. However, for the first time, in the rite entitled "The Blessing of an abbot or abbess," we find mention of an oath of fidelity. It occurs at the end of Mass and is done on the altar. This act done at this time and upon the altar will become much more important in the Pontifical of William Durandus.

---

[27] Andrieu, *Le Pontifical Romain,* 1:295–6.

"After mass is finished, the abbot stands before the pontiff, or another chosen by the pontiff, and makes an oath of fidelity upon the altar (*super altare iuramentum fidelitatis*) and gives a sign of peace to the one receiving the oath."[28]

This text is very important because, in its simplicity, it begins the ritual process of asking such an oath of all abbots and abbesses. What is even more important is the use of the term "oath," a term not yet used for the promises of obedience made by bishops or archbishops.

PERTINENT CONCILIAR TEXTS OF THE TWELFTH AND THIRTEENTH CENTURIES: THE RELATIONSHIP BETWEEN MONKS AND BISHOPS

We have already mentioned in chapter 2 the text from the First Lateran Council (1123), which emphasized the authority of the local bishop over the ministry of the presbyters in his diocese, such that presbyters ordained by the bishop's own hand are preferred. This same text, speaking of monks and obedience, confirms the connection between humility and obedience that has been evident in many of the texts already studied:

"Following in the footsteps of the holy fathers, we order by general decree, that monks be subject to their own bishops with all humility (*ut monachi propriis episcopis cum omni humilitate subiecti exsistant*), and show due obedience and devoted submission to them in all things (*debitam oboedientiam et devotam in omnibus subiectionem exhibeant*), as if to masters and shepherds of the church of God."[29]

This text, especially the last line, also seems to be influenced by wording in the promises of obedience in ordination rites, particularly the one for bishops in the Romano-Germanic Pontifical, "to exhibit in all things fidelity and subservience." What we seem to have here is part of the result of the Gregorian Reform or the Investiture Controversy.[30] With the emergence of a much stronger episcopacy, local monasteries came under either the local bishop or the papacy. In either case the relationship to the local bishop of the monk who had also

---

[28] Andrieu, *Le Pontifical Romain*, 2:413.
[29] Tanner, *Decrees of the Ecumenical Councils*, 1:193.
[30] O'Malley, "Priesthood, Ministry, and Religious Life," 230.

been ordained presbyter began to take on the ramifications of obedience as ritualized in ordination rites.

Important to our study are two texts from the Fourth Lateran Council (1215). The first, Canon 12, demanded that the local bishop hold every three years a general chapter of those abbots and priors who are not exempt.[31] It also called for the visitation of the monasteries by the local bishop on a regular basis. The second text, Canon 13, prohibited the founding of new orders because the great variety of religious orders leads to grave confusion in God's Church.[32] Thus anyone who wanted to become a religious should enter one of the already approved orders, and anyone who wanted to found a new order should follow the Rule of an already approved order. The rationale for the prohibition of new orders was due to the rise of heretical sects at this time. This is why Innocent III (1198–1216) had the Dominicans follow the rule of Augustine. However, with the Franciscans, this was not the case. Thus this canon was not always followed.[33]

THE DOMINICANS

We turn now to the founding of the mendicants, specifically the Dominicans and the Franciscans, and their rituals of profession. While approved by Innocent III shortly before his death in 1216, the Order of Preachers was first confirmed by Honorius III (1216–27) with the bulls of December 22, 1216, and January 21, 1217.[34] When we study their rite of profession, we are struck by four things, the emphasis of obedience, the relationship between "I make a profession" and "I promise obedience," the emphasis of promising obedience to the person who is the master general, and the change to the vassal ritual of the joining of hands.

"The manner of making a profession is as follows. I Brother N. make a profession and promise obedience (*facio professionem & promitto obedientiam*) to God and to Blessed Mary and Blessed Dominic and to you N. Master General of the Order of Friar Preachers and your successors

---

[31] Tanner, *Decrees of the Ecumenical Councils*, 1:240–1.

[32] Ibid., 242.

[33] H. Wolter in Jedin, *Handbook of Church History*, 4:171–81.

[34] Ibid., 174. A Spanish translation of both bulls may be found in Galmes and Gomez, *Santo Domingo de Guzmán*, 798–805.

according to the rule of Blessed Augustine and the Institutions of the Friar Preachers, that I will be obedient *(ero obediens)* to you and to your successors until I die."[35]

There is no longer any doubt about the importance of obedience in the order of things for the Dominicans, and while the Rule is still central, more central is the personal promise of obedience to the master general and his successors. The master general is mentioned twice, and one is to be obedient to him until death.

The relationship between "I make a profession" and "I promise obedience" is significant. *Professio* seems to include the entire life commitment of the brother. It is part of his spirituality and faith and is a broader term than the promise of obedience, which here is very specific and direct.

The promise of obedience is enhanced with the addition of the ritual of the joining of hands. The ceremony is described as follows:

"Then the novice genuflects before the Prior and the Prior takes the hands of the novice between his hands. The book of the Constitution is placed upon their hands and he who makes the profession reads: I Brother N., etc."[36]

It seems that the ritual of *immixtio manuum* in monasteries began with the Cluny reform. Here dependant priories were run by priors who took oaths of loyalty into the hands of their abbots like vassals.[37] This ritual was incorporated into the Rule of Augustine in the twelfth century, where now all monks took such an oath into the hands of their abbots with the following:

"Do you promise obedience to God and to me *(Promittis obedientiam Deo et mihi)* and to this holy congregation and perseverance in your stability *(perseverantiam stabilitatis tuae)* until death according to the grace conferred upon you by God and to the extent of your strength? I Promise."[38]

---

[35] Holste, *Codex Regularum Monasticarum et Canonicarum,* vol. 4, Graz, 46.

[36] Ibid., 216.

[37] Kempf in Jedin, *Handbook of Church History,* 3:325.

[38] de Aspurz, "Il rito della professione nell'ordine Francescano," 248–9. Kleinheyer, *Die Priesterweihe im Römischen Ritus,* 215. The text is from the Canons Regular of San Vittore as found in Martène, *De Antiquis Ecclesiae Ritibus Libri,* 3:743.

Here we see the vestige of promises in the *Rule of Benedict*. However, obedience is again emphasized, along with stability to the congregation, but conversion is omitted. It seems that it is this ritual that was incorporated into the above Dominican ritual.

To understand the significance of the change from a profession made upon the altar to a profession made in the joining of hands[39] and the rationale for monasteries to incorporate this feudal ritual into their ceremonies, we recall that the necessity for order demanded it. This was a way of ritualizing one's commitment. They simply took what had been part of society and made it theirs. Many diocesan presbyters made such a promise, although the *immixtio manuum* was not intrinsic to the rite of ordination of presbyters and would not be added to it until the Pontifical of William Durandus.

This promise done in the joining of hands had the advantage of symbolizing a reciprocal relationship, while the promise upon the altar is by nature unilateral. In this sense it is a richer symbol of the nature of obedience as relational.

Finally, the emphasis on obedience needs to be understood in the greater context of the juridical practice of obedience at this time in terms of both ordination rites of presbyters and the relationship between the pope and all orders.[40] Since the *immixtio manuum* becomes part of the ordination rites for presbyters in the Pontifical of William Durandus in less than a century, it would seem that the *immixtio manuum* in the rites of profession of the various monastic and mendicant orders, at least in terms of its ritual connection to a promise of obedience, influenced the Pontifical of William Durandus.[41] It is important to remember that generally Dominicans as well as most other mendicants and monks were ordained presbyters, thus, the strong connection to obedience as envisioned in ordination rites. Nevertheless, it is more accurate to understand the ritual relationship of the promises of obedience as celebrated by mendicants and diocesan presbyters as reciprocal, with the rites mutually influencing each other.

[39] Pulickal, "Study of the Rite of Religious Profession," 55–8.
[40] A. Thomas, "La profession religieuse des Dominicains," 22–3; de Aspurz, "Il rito della professione nell'ordine Francescano," 252.
[41] de Aspurz sees the mendicants as imitating the ordination rite for presbyters, Il rito della professione nell'ordine Francescano," 250.

THE FRANCISCANS

The original Rule of the Franciscans presented to Innocent III is not extant. The first Rule we have is the *First Rule (Regula Prima)*. It is more scriptural in nature. More important is the *Second Rule (Regula Secunda)* or *Scrolled Rule (Regula bullata)* of 1223, which is more juridical in character and became the fundamental law of the Franciscans.[42] The most important aspect of this Rule is that it is a new rule, contrary to Canon 13 of the just finished Fourth Lateran Council. The second aspect is its vocabulary. Here for the first time we find "obedience and respect," which is to become part of the wording of the promise of obedience in the ordination rite for presbyters in the Pontifical of William Durandus. Likewise, in its juridical language we find "proceeding according to law" *(canonice intrantibus)*, which is part of the profession made by archbishops to the pope, which we found in the Roman pontificals of the twelfth century.[43] Here are those parts of the text important to our study:

"The Rule and life of the Friars Minor is this, to observe the holy Gospel of our Lord Jesus Christ by living in obedience, without property and in chastity *(in obedientia, sine proprio, & in castitate)*. Brother Francis promises obedience and reverence *(promittit obedientiam, & reverentiam)* to the lord Pope Honorius and his successors lawfully succeeding *(canonice intrantibus)* and to the Roman Church. And the other brothers are held to obey *(obedire)* brother Francis and his successors.

". . . When the year of probation is finished, they shall be received to obedience, promising to follow this life always and to keep the Rule *(ad obedientiam, promittenter vitam istam semper & Regulam observare)*.

". . . In addition I order the ministers on obedience *(per obedientiam)* to seek from the lord Pope one of the cardinals of the Holy Roman Church, who may be governor, protector and corrector of this brotherhood, to the end that we be always submissive and subject to the Holy Roman Church *(ut semper subditi, & subjecti pedibus ejusdem sanctae Ecclesiae)*, firm in the Catholic faith, and always observe poverty, humility and the holy Gospel of Our Lord Jesus Christ, as we have firmly promised *(firmiter promissimus)*."[44]

---

[42] Wolter in Jedin, *Handbook of Church History*, 4:178. Both texts may be found in Holste, *Codex Regularum Monasticarum et Canonicarum*, 3:22–33. An English translation of the *Regula Secunda* may be found in Brooke, *Coming of the Friars*, 120–5.

[43] Andrieu, *Le Pontifical Romain*, 1:290–1.

[44] Holste, *Codex Regularum Monasticarum et Canonicarum*, 3:30–3.

As with the Dominicans obedience is emphasized, but here we have a new set of three elements: "in obedience, without property, and in chastity." Francis promises obedience and reverence to the pope while the brothers promise obedience to Francis and his successors. While the Rule is mentioned, it is to be followed by living the gospel. This is part of the Franciscan charism of the evangelical life.[45] One unique structure of their notion of obedience was the request for a cardinal protector, who would govern and correct the brothers so they would be "always submissive and subject to the holy Church." This was part of the common language of obedience used at the time.[46]

We have an early example of Franciscan vows dating from 1260. We can call these "vows" because the verb "to vow" is used:

"I brother N., vow and promise (*Ego frater N., voveo et promitto*) to God and the Blessed Virgin Mary and blessed Francis and all the saints and you, Father, for the entirety of my life to serve the rule of the friars minor confirmed by lord Pope Honorius, by living in obedience, without property and in chastity (*vivendo in obedientia, sine proprio et in castitate*)."[47]

This is the first time we find the verb "to vow." It recalls the rich nuptial images of some of the prayers for the consecrated life that we studied earlier in the Romano-Germanic Pontifical. The promises for mendicant life are now seen in the context of the vows of consecrated life. The promise is made to the local head of the order, and it is to serve the Rule, which now consists of a new trinity of elements: "obedience, without property, and in chastity."

Finally, we have one more fact of early Franciscan life to note. In 1331 the minister general of the Franciscans made several ritual adaptations at the general council of Perpignano. One of these changes was the moving of the profession to Communion time as a ritual connection to the Eucharist.[48] This predates the Jesuit structure by some two hundred years and seems to parallel the postcommunion rite in

[45] O'Malley, "Priesthood, Ministry, and Religious Life," 230–5.
[46] For example, "osculatis primum pedibus pontificis" as found in the rite of ordination of presbyters in the Pontifical of the Roman Curia of the 13th Century, Andrieu, *Le Pontifical Romain*, 2:349.
[47] de Aspurz, "Il rito della professione nell'ordine Francescano," 254.
[48] Ibid., 259–60.

the rite of ordination of presbyters in the Pontifical of the Roman Curia of the thirteenth century, the "making a confession," which we studied in chapter 2.[49]

More importantly, concerning the relationship between this ritual move and the placement of the promise of obedience in the ordination rite of presbyters after Communion in the Pontifical of William Durandus, we can conclude that since the Pontifical of William Durandus was compiled in the late thirteenth century and thus predates this Franciscan council, this Franciscan move was probably influenced by changes in the rites of ordinations for presbyters.

In summation, we find the developments of mendicant promises and promises of obedience in ordination rites for presbyters to be mutually dependent. They influenced each other because of their mutual ministry as presbyters. It seems that the ritual of the joining of hands came to the rites of ordination from the monasteries and mendicants. It also seems that the placing of such promises at or after Communion is a development that began in ordination rites for presbyters.

THE PONTIFICAL OF WILLIAM DURANDUS

In the Pontifical of William Durandus we find a rite entitled "Becoming a monk or other religious," a ritual reminder that by this time we have numerous monastic orders as well as other canons and orders. From the title it also seems that at this time monks, canons, and mendicants were considered to be similar enough to be covered by a single ritual. This rite contains the same list of prayers found in the previous pontificals for the making of monks.

The next rite, "The profession of novices," is an elaborate rite of profession. It contains the following promise, which is made after the offertory:

"I, brother so and so *(Ego, frater talis)* offer myself to this monastery and promise to you *(promitto tibi),* the superior of this monastery and your successors according to law *(canonice intrantibus)* the obedience and respect owed *(obedientium* [sic] *et reverentiam debitam)* according to the canonical rule of this saint or order. I also promise to you *(Promitto etiam tibi)* and this congregation, those here present and those future members, that I will observe perpetual abstinence *(me*

[49] Andrieu, *Le Pontifical Romain,* 2:350.

perpetuo servaturum continentiam), as human frailty permits, and sta-
bililty of place, correction of life's habits and the renunciation of property *(atque stabilitatem in loco et morum emendationem et renuntio
propriis)."*[50]

The influence of mendicant promises is evident. The use of
"brother," "I promise to you," "according to law," and "obedience
and respect" are all borrowed from mendicant promises. This is an indication of the growth and spiritual influence of the mendicants.

Second, what is striking is the change in both the order and importance of the three elements of the *Rule of Benedict*. Obedience is mentioned first and is the heart of this promise, which seems to reflect the
similar development of the importance of obedience in mendicant
promises. The second element is a new one, abstinence, or a life of
self-denial. Finally, we find stability, followed by a new expression for
conversion, correction of life's habits, or a correction of one's lifestyle,
a clearer but harsher term. These three elements are dependent on the
Rule of Benedict and do not reflect some of the new elements developed by the mendicants except for the importance of obedience.

Third, this is an oral promise but is read from a paper. It is not in
the form of a "will you–I will" examination. After it is read, it is
placed on the altar. Thus the concept of the petition being read and
placed on the altar is maintained. There is no mention of signing anything. What is likewise significant is that there is no joining-of-the-
hands ritual, which seems to indicate that at least some of the
monastic orders, and certain orders other than the mendicants, had
not at this time universally accepted that ritual. This maintaining of
the "I promise" form seems to have influenced the return to the
promitto form of the promise of obedience for presbyters in the rite of
ordination for presbyters in this pontifical.[51]

Fourth, and most important, we have for the first time an explicit
promise made to the person of the abbot or prelate. This, "I promise
to you," is a very different concept of a monastic promise. In fact, the
wording is dependent on the mendicant promises. Likewise, the
wording seems to be dependent on the stronger role now played by
obedience in this rite. No longer is obedience understood simply as a

---

[50] Andrieu, *Le Pontifical Romain*, 3:399.
[51] Ibid., 372.

personal aspect of monastic or religious life. It now has a canonical aspect, *according to law*, which parallels its ritual role in the ordination rite for presbyters. Thus it seems that the juridical aspect of obedience in the ordination rites for presbyters is present here, since generally at this time most monks and members of canons and orders were ordained presbyters.

This bring us to the fifth and final point. The brother promises "obedience and respect" to his abbot or prelate. These same terms are found for the first time in the promise of obedience in the rite of ordination for presbyters in this Pontifical of William Durandus. This is an indication of the reciprocal influence of the juridical notion of obedience in orders finding its way into monastic profession and vice versa.

Now we turn to the rite entitled "The confirmation and blessing of a regular abbot." The title indicates this rite is for those abbots under episcopal control. This helps to remind us that this pontifical was compiled for the local bishops, and thus its use was not expected in exempt abbeys. Here for the first time we have a full *examinatio* in *vis-volo* form. The first and final questions are significant.

"Will you observe your sacred purpose and the rule of saint Benedict *(Vis tuum sanctum propositum et sancti Benedicti regulam observare)* and diligently instruct those subject to you that they might do the same? Resp.: I will.

"Will you devotedly and with perpetual fidelity exhibit *(devote ac fideliter perpetuo exhibere)* to this holy church of Mende (Mimatensi) to me its bishop and to my successors fidelity, subservience, obedience and respect *(fidem, subiectionem, obedientiam et reverentiam)?* Resp.: I will."[52]

The significance of "purpose" we have already mentioned. It is the abbot's special spousal responsibility to observe the Rule and teach his monks to do likewise. Most important, here for the first time we have a promise of obedience made by the abbot to the local church, here Mimatensis (or Mende), and its bishop and his successors. What is curious is the slight change in wording between this promise and the one made by a newly ordained suffragan bishop to his metropolitan in this pontifical.

[52] Ibid., 401–2.

"Will you exhibit to blessed Peter . . . and to the holy church of Bituricae (Bituricensi) and to me its minister and my successors fidelity, subservience and obedience according to canonical authority *(fidem, subiectionem et obedientiam secundum canonicam auctoritatem)?*"[53]

In both questions we have the mention of the local church. In the question for abbots we have the addition of "respect." We have already noted the use of "respect" as coming from the wording of Franciscan promises. Second, "according to canonical authority" is replaced with "with devoted and perpetual fidelity." It would seem that this change must be understood as part of the response to the Investiture Controversy. The desire was that monasteries be under either papal or episcopal control, and this is one ritual expression of that desire.

The abbot then makes the following promise:

"I, N., ordinary abbot or abbess of this monastery, promise before God and his holy ones *(promitto, coram Deo et sanctis eius)* and the brothers (sisters) of this solemn congregation fidelity, worthy subservience, obedience and respect *(fidelitatem dignamque subiectionem, obedientiam et reverentiam)* to my mother this church, to you N., my lord and the bishop of this church and to your successors, according to the statutes of the sacred canons *(secundum sacrorum statuta canonum)* just as the inviolable authority of the Roman Pontiffs command. And this I affirm with an oath with my own hand upon this altar or upon this holy Gospel of God *(Et hec manu propria super hoc altare vel super hec sacrosancta Dei evangelia iureiurando firmo).* May God and this holy Gospel help me."[54]

First of all, we read that this promise is for both abbots and abbesses. It is an amalgamation of the older Benedictine promises with influences from mendicant promises and the rite of ordination for bishops.[55] In fact, it has similarities to the promise made by bishops in this pontifical,[56] except that the bishops make their promise "upon the altar and upon the book of the gospels" while the abbots

[53] Ibid., 379.
[54] Ibid., 402.
[55] Aubry, "A propos de la signification du 'Promitto,'" 1064.
[56] Andrieu, *Le Pontifical Romain*, 3:392.

can make it either "upon the altar" or "upon the gospel." Finally, as in the Pontifical of the Roman Curia of the thirteenth century,[57] it takes on the language of an oath: "I affirm with an oath." It is curious that the promise for bishops has not yet taken on such language.

In summation, the most significant issues of the Pontifical of William Durandus is that for the first time we have abbots and abbesses making oaths of fidelity to the local bishops. While this seems to be the result of the Investiture Controversy, what is more important is that by Trent all promises by bishops to the pope will likewise be called oaths. Thus the use of this more juridical term has its beginnings in the blessings of abbots and abbesses.

Second, these monastic rituals have been deeply influenced by vocabulary from both the mendicants and ordination rites. This is the result of the growth in the juridical notion of obedience, which in itself is a result of the reality that most monks and mendicants were ordained presbyters.

Finally, for the first time we have the explicit promising of obedience by monks to the person of the abbot in the rite of profession. Now the structure is completely hierarchical, monk to abbot, abbot to bishop or pope, just as in the diocesan structure of presbyter to bishop and bishop to pope. This seems to be part of a desire for ritual symmetry, or a certain similarity between rituals concerning similar entities. This will become most obvious in the Tridentine reform.

PERTINENT CONCILIAR TEXTS OF THE SIXTEENTH CENTURY: THE RELATIONSHIP BETWEEN MENDICANTS AND BISHOPS

The most remarkable aspect of the mendicant orders was their papal exemption, which was very different from the exemption enjoyed by Cluny and other exempt abbeys. While Cluny, Citeaux, and other abbeys were granted freedom in favor of the interior development of the monastery, the mendicants were granted freedom for a particular kind of ministry. Their ministry, for the reform of the Church, was granted freedom from local episcopal interference precisely because of the nature of that reform.[58] Thus the mendicants were able to expand quickly, preach everywhere, and teach at many

---

[57] Ibid., 2:413.
[58] O'Malley, "Priesthood, Ministry, and Religious Life," 235–7.

of the great universities, resulting in an influence far beyond any previous reform movement.

What is of interest, however, is the development of the relationship between these mendicants and local bishops over the next few centuries. By the time we arrive at the Fifth Lateran Council (1512–17) we have texts that speak of a certain tension and disquiet between mendicants and the local bishops. These texts are very detailed and seem to speak to the discord by calling for unity and charity. However, the basic teaching is that the authority of the local bishop is to be kept intact whenever there is a conflict with the mendicants.

"The exercise of spiritual rights, which concern the glory of God and the salvation of the souls of Christ's faithful, has been entrusted to bishops and their superiors in their dioceses, since they have chosen to be sharers of our burden, as we have already said, and since dioceses with defined boundaries have been assigned to each of the bishops. We truly desire, then, that these spiritual rights be exercised by the bishops, and that the right of freely exercising them be truly, as far as possible, kept intact for them. If our predecessors as Roman pontiffs and the apostolic see have granted any such spiritual rights to the said mendicant friars to the harm of the bishops, we consider that such concessions made to religious ought in future to be limited (*moderandas*), so that the friars themselves will be supported in all charity by the said bishops rather than be troubled and disturbed. For, regulars and seculars, prelates and subjects, exempt and non-exempt, belong to the one universal church, outside of which no one at all is saved, and they all have *one Lord and one faith.* That is why it is fitting that, belonging to the one same body, they also have the one same will; and just as the brethren are united by the bond of mutual charity, so it is not fitting that they arouse among themselves injustice and hurt, since the Saviour says, *My commandment is that you love one another as I have loved you.*"[59]

The key word here is "limited." Whatever privileges that had been granted and that now cause problems are to be limited. The text goes on to grant bishops the right to visit parishes run by mendicants and the right to examine friars before they are ordained or hear confes-

---

[59] Tanner, *Decrees of the Ecumenical Councils,* 1:646.

sions. Likewise friars are to be ordained by the local bishop or his deputy. They need consent from the pastor to bless marriages and to do a host of other rituals and ceremonies. This section closes with the following call to holy obedience:

"We warn *(monemus)* the friars, in virtue of holy obedience *(in virtute sanctae obedientiae)*, to revere bishops with fitting honour and due respect *(congruo honore et convenienti observantia venerentur)*, out of the reverence owed to us and the apostolic see *(pro debita et nostra ac apostolicae sedis reverentia)*, since they act as deputies *(subrogatos)* in place of the holy apostles."[60]

The key teaching here is that the bishops serve as deputies in the place of the apostles. Thus friars owe bishops obedience and the Apostolic See reverence. We see clearly the hierarchical structure in place. The great mendicant experiment, as with the great abbeys of an earlier time, is becoming part of this structure for the sake of unity and charity.

These structural teachings are strengthened in session 23 of the Council of Trent (July 15, 1563). Canon 10 prohibits abbots and others with whatever exemptions from conferring minor orders on anyone not subject to them without proper dimissorial letters. This right belongs to the local bishop "not withstanding any contrary privileges, prescriptions or customs however immemorial."[61] This is a clear statement of a new order of things.

Canon 12 deals with the age for major orders and declares that regulars, a term to encompass all orders, are not to be ordained too young or without careful examination by the bishop, closing with the phrase "all privileges in this matter are wholly ruled out."[62] This same type of phrasing follows the prohibition in Canon 13 of conferring two holy orders on the same person on the same day, even on regulars. Canon 15 repeats the demand that the bishop examine and approve confessors, again with the same phrasing, to nullify all previous exemptions and privileges. All in all, the teachings of Trent signal the further centralization of power in the papacy and episcopacy.

[60] Ibid., 649.
[61] Ibid., 2:748.
[62] Ibid., 749.

In summation, we can just reiterate the strengthening of the juridical aspects of obedience, such that local bishops came to have much more control over both monasteries and mendicants in their dioceses. These juridical aspects of obedience, which we studied in the above conciliar texts, will be reflected in the further ritualization of obedience in the Tridentine reform. This, perhaps, is a historical development that continues today with the most recent addition of a promise of obedience for religious priests to the local bishop found in the 1990 *Editio typica altera.*

PONTIFICALE ROMANUM OF 1596

In the Roman Pontifical of 1596 we have a simple rite, "The Blessing of an Abbot," which has no oaths or promises. The next rite, "The Blessing of an Abbot by Apostolic authority," contains both an oath of fidelity and an *examinatio,* which includes a promise of obedience. This rite concerns territorial abbots. To indicate that we have now finally completed the ritual symmetry between bishops and abbots, the form for making the oath for abbots is exactly the same as for bishops except that the long section on *ad limina* visits for bishops is left out.[63]

Then we come to the *examinatio.* As in the Pontifical of William Durandus, the first and final questions are important. However, we now have two forms for the final question, one for exempt abbeys and an extra one for those abbeys under local episcopal control.

"Will you observe your sacred purpose *(tuum sanctum propositum),* and the rule of saint N. *(sancti N. regulam),* and diligently instruct those subject to you that they might do the same? I will.

"Will you devotedly and with perpetual fidelity exhibit in all things *(per omnia)* to the holy Roman Church and our most holy lord N., the most high Pontiff, and his successors fidelity, subservience, obedience and respect *(fidem, subiectionem, obedientiam, et reverentiam)?* I will.

"Will you devotedly and with perpetual fidelity exhibit to the holy Church N., its Patriarch or Archbishop or Bishop, and my successors fidelity, subservience, obedience and respect? I will."[64]

The first question is exactly the same as that of the Pontifical of William Durandus except that the particular name of the Rule is added.

[63] *Pontificale Romanum,* 101–2.
[64] Ibid., 103.

The final question is likewise the same as that of the Pontifical of William Durandus except that "in all things" is added, again reflecting symmetry with the Tridentine wording for the promise for bishops.

In summation, the most important ritual element evident in the *Pontificale Romanum* is that ritual symmetry is finally reached between the rite of consecration for bishops and the blessing of abbots in terms of the wording for the oaths of fidelity and promises of obedience. While there is still the distinction between exempt and non-exempt abbeys, the vocabulary is the same. Thus, in terms of ritual and jurisdiction the rites for bishops and abbots reflect the same hierarchical structure toward which both our conciliar texts and pontifical rituals have been heading. Finally, for the first time the written promises of fidelity made by both bishops and abbots are called oaths. The only major ritual element not present in the *Pontificale Romanum* is the connection of this oath to the altar. This seems to be due to the fact that these oaths were seen as extrinsic to the ritual of consecration, a fact we pointed out in our study of the consecration of bishops in chapter 2.

CONCLUSIONS

First, there was a reciprocal exchange of vocabularies between rites of profession and blessings of abbots and promises of obedience in ordination rites, with the various rituals influencing one another. Second, as more and more monks were ordained presbyters and as mendicants were generally ordained presbyters, the juridical ramifications of the promise of obedience in ordination rites influenced their expression in rites of profession. Third, the ritual connection of the joining of hands to the rites of profession seems to predate its ritual inclusion in ordination rites. Fourth, the return to the use of "I promise" in the promises of obedience in ordination rites for presbyters seems to have been influenced by rites of profession. Fifth, the concept of a written promise and its connection to the altar, while not copied by the mendicants, remained to influence the oaths of fidelity taken by both abbots and bishops, including the use of the term "oath." Sixth, there is movement toward ritual symmetry, reflecting the larger movement toward papal and episcopal centralization of authority, resulting in very similar rituals for monks, mendicants, and diocesan presbyters on the one hand, and abbots and bishops on the other. This process continues up to our time.

4

The Second Vatican Council

Theologically, the Second Vatican Council is a unique council in the sense that it was called simply for a general renewal of the Church. There were no great heresies to combat. Things seemingly were at peace, and Catholics were generally pleased with the status quo.

However, there were major reform movements already operative in the Church. Much groundwork had been laid in general by the liturgical movement and new studies in Scripture and in particular by the papal writings of Pius XII, such as *Mystici Corporis, Mediator Dei,* and *Sacramentum Ordinis.*[1] *Mystici Corporis* in 1943 explored the mystery of the Church as the mystical body of Christ. *Mediator Dei* in 1947 dealt with the liturgical life of the Church and stressed Christ's presence and action. It actually set the stage for the final acts of the liturgical movement that bore fruit in the Second Vatican Council. *Sacramentum Ordinis* in 1947 settled the issue of the matter and form in the sacrament of orders to be the imposition of hands and the prayer of consecration. These studies allowed for a council that was transformed from within by its theologians, building on recent scholarship and a fuller understanding of the history and development of the traditions of the Church.

Concerning the sacrament of orders, the major theological development was the return to the patristic understanding of the bishop as possessing the fullness of priesthood[2] and the implications such a

[1] Osborne, *Priesthood,* 300–6.
[2] See the two articles by Ryan, "Episcopal Consecration: The Fullness of the Sacrament of Order," 293–324, and "Vatican II: The Rediscovery of the Episcopate," 208–41.

return would have on our theology of the priesthood.[3] One implication is the new theological understanding of the relationship between bishop and presbyter and how that relationship is worked out ritually and canonically. This working out of relationships must also include religious presbyters. A second implication is the continual theological development of the relationship between bishops as successors of the apostles and the pope as successor of Peter. Our understanding of both issues continues to develop and unfold, both ritually and canonically.

Finally, we need to focus on obedience and orders as it concerned the bishops and experts (periti) at the Second Vatican Council. Obedience was not an issue of concern in the preparatory work of the council.[4] While there were many major revisions in the documents that would eventually be passed, revisions that would invert our understanding of priesthood,[5] the concept of the promise of obedience in ordination rites was taken as a given and not even mentioned in the final versions of council documents, such as the Dogmatic Constitution on the Church (Lumen Gentium) or the Decree on the Ministry and Life of Priests (Presbyterorum Ordinis).[6] Rather, the theological understanding of the sacramental bond between bishop and presbyter sharing in the one priesthood of Christ was a far stronger focus than the canonical obligations of the promise of obedience.[7] Having said this, we turn to those texts of the Second Vatican Council that are pertinent to our study.

PERTINENT TEXTS OF THE SECOND VATICAN COUNCIL: THE RELATIONSHIP BETWEEN BISHOP, PRESBYTER, AND DEACON

The revision of orders as envisioned in The Constitution on the Sacred Liturgy (Sancrosanctum Concilium) 76 is meager. It simply calls for both the texts and the ceremonies of the rites of ordination to be re-

[3] See Osborne, *Priesthood*, 307–42; Nichols, *Holy Orders*, 131–41.

[4] Schneider, "Obedience to the Bishop," 76.

[5] For studies of textual revisions pertinent to our study see Joncas, "Recommendations Concerning Roman Rite Ordinations," 307–40; P. Cordes in Vorgrimler, *Commentary on the Documents of Vatican II*, 4:238–45; Schneider, "Obedience to the Bishop," 82–135.

[6] Schneider, "Obedience to the Bishop," 109–10.

[7] Ibid., 111. For a negative view of the theological implications of the new ordination rites see Coomaraswamy, "Post-Conciliar Rite of Holy Orders," 154–87.

vised. It allows for the allocutions and the words of ordination to be in the vernacular and for all bishops present at an episcopal consecration to lay hands.[8]

To enter into the theological issues that concern our study we must first turn to the Dogmatic Constitution on the Church *(Lumen Gentium)*. After speaking about the theological role of bishops (21–27), the text finally touches on presbyters and deacons in 28 and 29. Number 28 begins with a declaration that bishops share in the consecration and mission of Christ because they are successors of the apostles and that there are different divinely instituted orders in the Church called bishops, presbyters, and deacons. Then it speaks of presbyters *(presbyteri)*, which all our approved English editions translate as "priests." This is not quite accurate, as the term priests *(sacerdoti)* refers to both bishops and presbyters. Likewise, the term "priesthood" *(sacerdotium)* refers to the one priesthood of Christ to which all bishops and presbyters belong, while the term presbyterate *(presbyterium)* refers to the body of presbyters who, with their bishop, serve in a local church.[9] We will keep these terms distinct in our work with the various texts. With these points, here are the most important texts of *Lumen Gentium* 28:

"Although they do not possess the highest honour of the pontificate and depend on the bishops for the exercise of their power, *(in exercenda sua potestate ab Episcopis pendeant)*, priests *(presbyteri)* nevertheless are united with them in priestly honour, and by virtue of the sacrament of order they are consecrated in the image of Christ, the high and eternal priest. . . .

"As prudent cooperators of the episcopal order *(ordinis Episcopalis providi cooperatores)* and its instrument and help, priests *(presbyteri)* are called to the service of the people of God and constitute along with their bishop one presbyterium *(unum presbyterium cum suo Episcopo constituunt)* though destined to different duties. . . .

"Because of this sharing in the priesthood *(sacerdotio)* and mission, priests *(presbyteri)* are to recognise the bishop as truly their father and reverently obey him *(eique reverenter oboediant)*. The bishop, for his part, is to consider the priests *(sacerdotes)* his cooperators *(cooperatores suos)* as sons and friends. . . .

[8] Tanner, *Decrees of the Ecumenical Councils*, 2:834.
[9] See Power, "The Basis for Official Ministry in the Church," 60–88.

"By reason, therefore, of order and ministry *(ratione Ordinis et minis-terii),* all priests both diocesan and religious *(omnes sacerdotes, tum dioecesani tum religiosi)* are associated *(coaptantur)* with the body of bishops *(corpori igitur episcoporum)* and according to their grace and vocation they work for the good of the whole church.

"By virtue of sacred ordination and the mission they have in common, all priests *(presbyteri)* are bound together in a close fraternity."[10]

Among the issues important to our study is the teaching that presbyters are *dependent* on the bishops for the faculties to function as presbyters. This is the traditional Tridentine understanding of the need for presbyters. This dependence is balanced with the teaching that presbyters and bishops share the honor of the one priesthood of Christ by virtue of their ordination.[11] Presbyters are *cooperators* with the bishops in their mission, the same mission all presbyters share in common. Nevertheless, presbyters *reverently obey* their bishops, an echo of the promise of obedience from the rite of ordination. There is also the reciprocal responsibility of the bishop to consider his presbyters as sons and friends. While this reciprocal concept is still weak, we will watch its development in various subsequent texts.

More importantly, we are given an image of the unity of all priests with the body of bishops. By reason of their order and ministry all priests, whether diocesan or religious, are associated with the body of bishops, and they are to work together for the good of the Church. This is not so much a canonical image as an ecclesial one, but one that is demanded by good ministry. Priesthood is nothing if it is not ordered to the service of the Church. However, the relationship between diocesan and religious presbyters, and how these relate to the local bishop, is yet to be worked out. This will be a major issue in the next chapter.

Finally, as in scholastic theology, we continue to have a dual source of priestly power, namely, order and jurisdiction. Here they take on different terms, such as "in priesthood and mission" and "in virtue of sacred ordination and mission," but the duality continues. Since this power is the one power of the priesthood of Christ,[12] perhaps more thought needs to be given to how this power is to be understood and

[10] Tanner, *Decrees of the Ecumenical Councils,* 872–3.
[11] A. Grillmeier in Vorgrimler, *Commentary on the Documents of Vatican II,* 1:223.
[12] J. Galot, *Theology of the Priesthood,* 186.

ritually and canonically expressed. The relationship between the ritual intent of the promise of obedience in ordination rites and the bishop's responsibility to oversee ministry in his diocese is the main issue here. Certainly faculties are given in order for presbyters to serve the needs of the people of a diocese, but do bishops think that the promise of obedience made by presbyters is a means to control the vision of ministry in their diocese?

Returning to our study of *Lumen Gentium*, chapter 29 simply speaks of deacons as those who stand at a lower rank of the hierarchy, "on whom hands are imposed 'not for the priesthood, but for the ministry.' . . . [T]hey are at the service of the people of God . . . in communion with the bishop and his presbyterium."[13] This keeps the traditional distinction that deacons are not ordained to the priesthood[14] but also includes the notion that deacons are to be of service to the presbyterate. While mentioning some of the many ministries a deacon can do and restoring the diaconate to a proper and permanent rank of the hierarchy, it leaves the working out of the theology and rituals for the order of deacon for a later time.

We turn now to the Decree on the Pastoral Office of Bishops in the Church (15) *(Christus Dominus)*, where we find a good theological summation of the relationships between bishop, presbyter, and deacon:

"For bishops enjoy the fullness of the sacrament of orders and priests *(presbyteri)* depend on them in the use of their power. These too have been ordained true priests *(sacerdotes)* of the new testament to be prudent assistants *(cooperatores)* of the episcopal order. Deacons likewise have been ordained for the ministry and serve the people of God in communion with their bishop and his priests *(presbyterio)*."[15]

Much of this text is a repeat of *Lumen Gentium* 28 and 29, which we just studied.

Christus Dominus 28 is directed to diocesan clergy, but its opening statement is most important:

---

[13] Tanner, *Decrees of the Ecumenical Councils*, 874.

[14] H. Vorgrimler in Vorgrimler, *Commentary on the Documents*, 1:228.

[15] Tanner, *Decrees of the Ecumenical Councils*, 926. For a study on the bishop as having the fullness of orders, see B. Cooke, "Fullness of Orders: Theological Reflections," in Provost, *Official Ministry in a New Age*, 151–67.

"All priests, whether diocesan or religious *(Omnes quidem presbyteri sive dioecesani sive religiosi),* together with the bishop share in and exercise the one priesthood of Christ *(unum sacerdotium Christi cum Episcopo participant et exercent),* and are, therefore, ordained to be prudent cooperators *(cooperatores)* of the episcopal order."[16]

Again, much of this vocabulary is a repeat of *Lumen Gentium.* Most important is the use of the term "diocesan presbyters." This is a new term giving a new understanding to presbyters incarnated in a diocese. The text includes all presbyters, diocesan and religious, in the one priesthood of Christ, but the exercise of which is dependent on the local bishop. However, this relationship between religious presbyters and the local bishop is not clear.[17]

Christus Dominus 34 and 35 does clarify this relationship.[18] First, all religious priests are, like their diocesan brothers, cooperators with the episcopal order. All religious should always show loyal respect and reverence for the bishops as successors of the apostles. Then we come to the section on the privilege of exemption:

"The privilege of exemption, by which religious are assigned to the service of the supreme pontiff or to some other ecclesiastical authority and are withdrawn from the jurisdiction of the bishops, has in view principally the internal order of the institutes. The object is that everything in these institutes should be well coordinated and in the interest of the growth and perfection of religious life. The purpose of exemption is also that the supreme pontiff may be able to use these religious for the good of the whole church, or indeed that some other competent authority may be able to use them for the good of churches under its own jurisdiction. This exemption, however, does not stand in the way of religious in their respective dioceses coming canonically under the jurisdiction of the bishops, in so far as is required for the fulfillment of their pastoral duties and the well ordered care of souls."[19]

[16] Ibid., 932.
[17] K. Mörsdorf in Vorgrimler, *Commentary on the Documents,* 2:255–6. For an excellent discussion of the issues here, see O'Malley, "Priesthood, Ministry, and Religious Life," 248–57.
[18] Tanner, *Decrees of the Ecumenical Councils,* 934–6.
[19] Ibid., 935.

What is very clear here, after the purpose of exemption is defined, is that all pastoral activity is under the jurisdiction of the local bishop. What falls subject to the authority of the local bishop is further clarified in the next section. Here, divine worship, preaching, the care of souls, religious education, and so on, indeed, all public ministry, is under the authority of the local bishop. There is little doubt as to the inclusion of the pastoral ministry of all religious under local episcopal jurisdiction.

Next we turn to the Decree on the Ministry and Life of Priests *(Presbyterorum Ordinis)*, which was one of the documents that underwent numerous major revisions.[20] This was one of the last documents approved at the end of the last session; thus it shows some of the inconsistencies evident in a text filled with compromises and given hurried treatment.[21] Number 7 contains the following texts, which are significant:

"All priests *(presbyteri)* share with bishops in one and the same priesthood *(sacerdotium)* and ministry of Christ, but in such a way that the very unity of their consecration and mission requires their hierarchical communion with the order of bishops; this they fittingly express by concelebrating from time to time in the liturgy, and by proclaiming that it is in union with them that they celebrate the eucharistic meal. . . .

"Priests *(Presbyteri)* for their part, bearing in mind the fullness of the sacrament of order given to bishops, should respect *(revereantur)* in them the authority of Christ the supreme shepherd. They should be loyal to their own bishop with true love and obedience. *(Suo igitur Episcopo sincera caritate et oboedientia adhaereant.)* Such obedience on the part of priests *(Quae sacerdotalis oboedientia)* is permeated with a spirit of cooperation *(cooperationis spiritu perfusa),* and is founded on that very sharing in the episcopal ministry which is conferred on them through the sacrament of order and their canonical mission *(missionem canonicam)*."[22]

First of all, the unity of the priesthood is colored with the issues of the newly restored concept of concelebration; thus it is less focused than the similar passages from *Lumen Gentium* we have just studied.

[20] Osborne, *Priesthood,* 308–15; Cordes in Vorgrimler, *Commentary on the Documents,* 4:238.

[21] Schneider, "Obedience to the Bishop," 132–3.

[22] Tanner, *Decrees of the Ecumenical Councils,* 1050–2.

Likewise the vocabulary concerning obedience is less focused, especially the statement that priestly obedience is permeated with a spirit of cooperation, which seems to give obedience a more pastoral slant.[23] However, we have a new element with mission being defined as canonical. This seems to imply the dependence on the bishop for the power to function as a presbyter, which we read in *Lumen Gentium*. And as we read in *Lumen Gentium*, we continue to have a dual source of priestly power, that is, by virtue of orders and by virtue of sharing in the mission of Christ. This simply continues the scholastic distinction of order and jurisdiction, the implications of which need further thought.[24]

Finally, we turn to the understanding of obedience in the context of priestly ministry. We continue with *Presbyterorum Ordinis* 15, where obedience is placed in the context of hierarchical communion and is understood as leading to a more mature freedom for those who serve.

"As a ministry of the church, the priestly ministry *(ministerium autem sacerdotale)* can only be fulfilled in the hierarchical communion of the whole body. Pastoral love therefore impels priests *(presbyteros)*, in the exercise of that communion, to devote their own will, in obedience, *(voluntatem propriam per oboedientiam)* to the service of God and their fellow human beings, accepting and putting into effect in a spirit of faith whatever is enjoined or recommended by the supreme pontiff and their own bishop, or other superior. . . .

"This obedience leads to a more natural freedom in the sons of God. *(Haec oboedientia, quae ad maturiorem libertatem filiorum Dei adducit)."*[25]

"Obedience" here seems to mean "to think with the Church," but this is a little idealistic. It passes by certain problems such as the right use of authority. Likewise, there is no mention of the reciprocal relationship between subordinates and superiors. Finally, the concept of the mature freedom of the sons of God is proclaimed without much explanation of what such an idea implies.[26]

Some of these ideas seem to have come from the Decree on the Up-to-Date Renewal of Religious Life *(Perfectae Caritatis)* 14, passed just a

[23] Cordes in Vorgrimler, *Commentary on the Documents*, 4:244.

[24] Osborne, *Priesthood*, 338. He puts the *missio canonica* in the context of the three-fold office of bishop and priest.

[25] Tanner, *Decrees of the Ecumenical Councils*, 1061.

[26] F. Wulf in Vorgrimler, *Commentary on the Documents*, 4:277–9.

few months earlier. Here religious obedience is understood as leading to freedom and maturity, but for the first time the powers of superiors are limited, as they are called to be responsible for their subjects.[27]

"Through the vow of obedience, religious *(Religiosi per professionem oboedientiae)* surrender to God in self-sacrifice the free determination of their lives. They conform themselves more authentically, more intimately to the saving design of God. They imitate Jesus Christ. . . .

"Obedience, therefore, increases the freedom of God's children; it is not destructive of human dignity, but actually realises personality more fully. *(Sic oboedientia religiosa, nedum dignitatem personae humanae minuit, illam, ampliata libertate filiorum Dei, ad maturitatem adducit).*

"Superiors, for their part, will have to answer for those for whom they are responsible (see Heb 13:17). They must be alert to God's will in the execution of their responsibilities; they must govern as the servants of their communities, reflecting the kindness that God himself offers them. They should treat their communities as daughters and sons of God, persons to be reverenced; they should elicit obedience in freedom. *(Subditos regant qua filios Dei et cum respectu personae humanae, illorum voluntariam subiectionem promoventes)."*[28]

Obviously, the first point is that religious obedience is directed toward serving God by following the example of Christ. This is a return to the pristine notion of obedience in the *Rule of Benedict* and early monasticism. Second, the notions of freedom, maturity, human dignity, and respect of the person are part of the reality of obedience for both religious by their profession and for diocesan presbyters by their ordination. The sanctity of the person is the same in both. Finally, the return of the understanding of obedience as a reciprocal relationship is very helpful. It parallels the pastoral images of a bishop, which we saw in *Lumen Gentium* 28, as one who cares for his presbyters and considers them his sons and friends. What is hinted at but not developed is the reality of possible abuse whereby a superior or bishop misuses his power over those obedient to him. We continue to

[27] F. Wulf in Vorgrimler, *Commentary on the Documents,* 2:363. For an excellent reflection on the contemporary issues of religious obedience, see Seasoltz, "Religious Obedience: Liberty and Law," 73–93.

[28] Tanner, *Decrees of the Ecumenical Councils,* 944.

struggle with those superiors who abuse their position of power. Thus this small development in a truly reciprocal notion of obedience must be treasured.

Before our summation of the pertinent texts of the Second Vatican Council, there is one more text to take into account, namely, Paul VI's first encyclical letter on the nature of the Church *(Ecclesiam Suam)*, dated August 6, 1964. Its subtitle is informative: "On the Ways in Which the Catholic Church Is To Pursue Its Mission in the Present Day." After dealing with the issues of the Church and the modern world, Paul VI concludes by discussing obedience in the final two sections:

"But this desire that the Church's internal relationships should take the form of a dialogue between members of a community founded upon love, does not mean that the virtue of obedience is no longer operative. . . .

"Moreover the very exercise of authority becomes, in the context of this dialogue, an exercise of obedience, the obedient performance of a service, a ministry of truth and charity. By obedience we mean the observance of canonical regulations and respect for the government of lawful superiors, but an observance and respect readily and serenely given, as is only to be expected from free and loving children.

"By contrast, a spirit of independence, bitter criticism, defiance, and arrogance is far removed from that charity which nourishes and preserves the spirit of fellowship, harmony, and peace in the Church. It completely vitiates dialogue, turning it into argument, disagreement and dissension—a sad state of affairs, but by no means uncommon. St. Paul warned us against this when he said: 'Let there be no schisms among you.'"[29]

This text gives an honest if rather negative portrayal of the struggles of living out obedience. These struggles are not new to the history of the Church. However, what is lacking is any sense of the relational aspect of obedience. The children, who are free and loving, are expected to be obedient. There is no reflection on the responsibility of the superior. This text demonstrates how hard it is for those in power to truly trust those subject to them. While speaking of the exer-

[29] *Acta Apostolicae Sedis* 56 (1964) 609-59. English translation: *The Pope Speaks* 10 (1964) 253–92.

cise of obedience as a dialogue, it is difficult to maintain a reciprocity that is meaningful.

In summation, we must acknowledge the development in the documents of the Second Vatican Council of the concept that presbyters are cooperators with the bishops in the priesthood of Christ, which the bishops possess in its fullness. This allows for a more reciprocal understanding of obedience, an obedience that can lead to a deeper maturity as sons of God. However, this is an ideal that is ever difficult to attain.[30]

Second, the council still struggles to conceptualize the power of the priesthood. If the scholastic terms of order and jurisdiction are really two aspects of the one power of the priesthood of Christ, how is that to be understood today? While jurisdiction was not emphasized, the concept of sharing in the mission of Christ and calling this mission canonical points to issues still to be clarified. Presbyters participate in the priesthood and mission of Christ, and in union with their bishop form one presbyterium. Yet they are dependent on their bishops for their canonical mission.

Third, with the council teaching that religious and diocesan presbyters alike share in the one priesthood of Christ, what is the relationship between those religious and the local bishop who represents the fullness of that priesthood? These are issues yet to be worked out.

Finally, the concept of a restored diaconate is still so new that very little was decided in the texts of the Second Vatican Council. This is a reality that is slowly developing in the decades following the council.

PERTINENT TEXTS FROM BOTH VATICAN COUNCILS: THE RELATIONSHIP BETWEEN BISHOPS AND THE POPE

Before proceeding to the actual study of the revision of the rites of ordinations subsequent to the Second Vatican Council, we must study those conciliar texts that reflect both the teachings and the tensions in the relationship between the local bishop, successor of the apostles, and the pope, successor of Peter. Both teachings and tensions will be reflected in the revision of the rite of ordination for bishops. The issue is not the primacy of the papacy. Rather, the issue is how that primacy relates to the dignity, power, and jurisdiction of each local bishop.

---

[30] See Müller, "Obedience to the Bishop," 79–88.

The First Vatican Council is properly known as the council that defined the infallibility of the pope. What is not so well known is its clear teaching on episcopal power in relation to papal authority. Here are the important sections from chapter 3 of *Pastor Aeternus* of that council:

"Wherefore we teach and declare that, by divine ordinance, the Roman church possesses a pre-eminence of ordinary power over every other church, and that this jurisdictional power of the Roman pontiff is both episcopal and immediate. . . .

"This power of the supreme pontiff by no means detracts from that ordinary and immediate power of episcopal jurisdiction, by which bishops, who have succeeded to the place of the apostles by appointment of the holy Spirit *(positi a Spiritu Sancto)*, tend and govern individually the particular flocks which have been assigned to them. On the contrary, this power of theirs is asserted, supported and defended by the supreme and universal pastor *(a supremo et universali pastore asseratur, roboretur ac vindicetur);* for St. Gregory the Great says: 'My honour is the honour of the whole church. My honour is the steadfast strength of my brethren. Then do I receive true honour, when it is denied to none of those to whom honour is due.'"[31]

What is clear is that local bishops are not mere legates of the pope. They too have ordinary and immediate power because they are successors of the apostles by appointment of the Holy Spirit. Their power is to be asserted, supported, and defended by the pope. How this tension is to be balanced is not described.

These same teachings and tensions are continued in the documents of the Second Vatican Council. We begin with the significant passages in *Lumen Gentium* 27:

"The bishops govern the churches entrusted to them as vicars and legates of Christ *(vicarii et legati Christi regunt).* . . .

"This power which they exercise personally in the name of Christ is proper, ordinary and immediate, although its exercise is ultimately controlled by the supreme authority of the church and can be circumscribed within certain limits for the good of the church or the faithful. . . .

[31] Tanner, *Decrees of the Ecumenical Councils*, 813–4.

"The pastoral office, that is to say the habitual and daily care of their sheep, is completely entrusted to the bishops and they are not to be considered vicars of the Roman pontiffs, because they exercise a power that is proper to themselves and most truly are said to be presidents *(antistites)* of the peoples they govern. Therefore their power is not destroyed *(non eliditur)* by the supreme and universal power, but on the contrary it is affirmed, strengthened and vindicated *(asseritur, roboratur et vindicatur)* by it, since the holy Spirit unfailingly preserves the form of government established in his church by Christ the lord."[32]

First of all, bishops are legates of Christ and not of the Roman pontiff. This is very clear. However, this authority can be limited for the good of the Church and the faithful. Then, by the repetition of the three verbs "affirmed, strengthened, and vindicated" from the text of the First Vatican Council, which describe how the pope is to support local bishops, we are told that episcopal authority is not destroyed or struck down *(non eliditur)* by papal authority. This is the most balanced statement of the tension between episcopal and papal power.

This tension is likewise stated in the Decree on the Pastoral Office of Bishops in the Church *(Christus Dominus)* 2–3, but it is not so balanced:

"The bishops also, assigned to their posititon by the holy Spirit *(positi a Spiritu Sancto),* take the place of the apostles as pastors of souls, and together with the supreme pontiff and under his authority *(una cum Summo Pontifice et sub Eiusdem auctoritate),* are sent to carry on the never-ending work of Christ, the eternal pastor. . . .

"The bishops, accordingly, through the holy Spirit who has been given to them, have been made true and authentic teachers of the faith, pontiffs and pastors *(veri et authentici effecti sunt fidei Magistri, Pontifices ac Pastores).*

"The bishops receive this episcopal function of theirs by being consecrated as bishops. They share in the solicitude for all the churches; and, in what pertains to teaching and pastoral government, they exercise their function over the whole church of God when they are united all together in one college or body in communion with and

---

[32] Ibid., 871.

under the authority of the supreme pontiff *(in communone et sub auc-toritate Summi Pontificis)*."[33]

Again we find part of the quote of the First Vatican Council. How-ever, not only is there no disclaimer of how papal authority does not infringe on episcopal authority, but instead we find bishops are now both one with the supreme pontiff and under his authority. The only balancing statement is the one that declares bishops to be true pontiffs and pastors. It seems this simple but profound statement concerning the dignity and equality of each bishop as a pontiff and pastor keeps the relationship between bishop and pope in its proper tension. It is in this context that we can sense the frustration that occurs when some curia officials of the Vatican question some of the decisions of various bishops or episcopal conferences. Furthermore, bishops are seen as a body, a college, and only in communion with this college and under its head can they function. Thus the issues of individual bishops and their relationship to the college of bishops under the authority of the pope remain.

Finally, the question of the process of the election of bishops needs to be mentioned here.[34] Could not the role of the local church and the bishops of the metropolitan area be enhanced? In this way the Petrine ministry of confirming his brothers would be better realized and bish-ops would better understand their communion with the college of bishops and the pope. Bishops would understand that they are true pontiffs and teachers because they have been in some way elected by their people and their fellow bishops and confirmed by the successor of Peter.

Returning to our texts, this same concept of bishops under the au-thority of the pope is found in *Christus Dominus* 11. After defining what a diocese is, individual bishops are defined:

"Individual bishops, to whom the pastoral care of particular churches has been committed, are the proper, official and immediate shepherds of these churches *(proprii, ordinarii et immediati earum pastores)*, under the authority of the supreme pontiff *(sub auctoritate Summi Pontificis)*.

[33] Ibid., 921.
[34] For a good summary of the recent history of papal appointments of bishops, see Sweeney, "The 'wound in the right foot': unhealed?" 207–34.

Accordingly they feed their sheep in the name of the Lord by fulfilling their office of teaching, sanctifying and governing them. At the same time, they themselves must recognise the rights that legitimately belong to patriarchs or to other hierarchic authorities."[35]

Here the phrase "under the authority of the supreme pontiff" is balanced with wording similar to *Lumen Gentium* 27. They are the "proper, official and immediate shepherds of these churches." A final balancing relationship is that of bishops to patriarchs or other hierarchs such as metropolitans.[36]

In summation, we must simply acknowledge the dignity and power of all bishops as successors to the apostles and the primacy of the pope as successor to Peter. While both Vatican councils struggled to keep these two entities in proper balance, the working out of this balance is still part of the major work to be done in future councils. Keeping this tension in mind, we can now turn to the revisions of ordination rites following the Second Vatican Council.

THE PROMISE OF OBEDIENCE IN THE REVISED RITES
FOR THE ORDINATION OF A DEACON, A PRESBYTER,
AND A BISHOP

The first obvious statement is the title. We continue the traditional rising order of deacon, presbyter, and bishop. Each is ordained. The traditional concept of bishops being consecrated is implied in the term "ordination." Finally, each is in the singular, a method reflecting the person to be ordained as opposed to any theological statement. The theological fruit of the teachings of the Second Vatican Council will not be reflected in this title until the revisions of the second typical edition of 1990 with the title *The Ordination of a Bishop, of Presbyters, and of Deacons.* Here the bishop is placed first, as presbyters and deacons are ordained into that one priesthood or ministry, and presbyters and deacons are plural to reflect the corporal reality of presbyters and deacons.

---

[35] Tanner, *Decrees of the Ecumenical Councils,* 924.
[36] Some of these tensions, especially the relationship between papal respresentatives, nuncios, etc., and the local bishops are discussed in Paul VI's apostolic letter "The Office of Papal Representatives" *(Sollicitudo omnium Ecclesiarum),* dated June 24, 1969. English translation: *The Pope Speaks* 14 (1969) 260–7.

As we look at the rites, we see that the first obvious change is that now for presbyters and deacons we have a new examination similar to the old one for bishops as part of the rite before the actual ordination. This *examinatio* also now contains a promise of obedience for both deacons and presbyters. Basically, this is a return to the order of the Romano-Germanic Pontifical, and the patterning of all three rites after the rite of ordination for bishops demonstrates a desire for ritual symmetry.[37] However, this new *examinatio* with its public character lends solemnity and weight to the candidate's commitment while also providing a new opportunity for a reciprocal expression of the ecclesial responsibilities of bishops, presbyters, and deacons.[38]

Part of the rationale of moving the promise of obedience for presbyters back to part of the *examinatio* before the actual ordination is that it makes more sense there. Likewise, the old postcommunion rite was not well ordered, especially the second laying on of hands for the power to forgive sins.[39] Finally, one of the few interjections from the bishops at the Second Vatican Council concerning the rite of ordinations came from Archbishop Armand Fares of Catanzaro-Sequillace, Italy, who called for a repositioning of the postcommunion rite to avoid duplication.[40]

The actual wording for the promise of obedience for both deacons and presbyters is exactly the same.

"Do you promise respect and obedience to me and my successors? *(Promittis mihi et successoribus meis reverentiam et oboedientiam?)* I do. *(Promitto)*.

"If the bishop is not the candidate's own Ordinary, he asks: Do you promise respect and obedience to your Ordinary? *(Promittis Ordinario Tuo reverentiam et oboedientiam?)* I do. *(Promitto.)*

[37] Kleinheyer, "Weiheliturgie in Neuer Gestalt," 225; Jounel, "La Nouveau Rituel D'Ordination," 69.

[38] Bugnini, *Reform of the Liturgy,* 719.

[39] Kleinheyer, "L'Ordination de Prêtres," 102–3.

[40] Joncas, "Recommendations Concerning Roman Rite Ordinations," 337. The text reads "Ultima pars ordinationis sacerdotalis fiat post orationes ultimas, seu orationes post antiphonam ad Postcomm., ne duplicata sint benedictio etc." Written interjections from Nov. 7, 1962, in *Acta Synodalia Sacrosancti Concilii Oecumenici Vaticani Secundi,* vol. 1 pars 2, p. 363.

"May God who has begun the good work in you bring it to fulfill-ment."[41]

This wording is also exactly the same as that of the Pontifical of William Durandus and the Tridentine rite.[42] It is curious that the entire *examinatio* for both deacons and presbyters is in the traditional "Will you–I will" form except for the promise of obedience, which is in the "Do you promise–I promise" form. It is also interesting that the official English translation chose to translate *promitto* with the simple "I do."

Likewise, the rite calls for this promise of obedience to be done in the vassalage form of the deacon or presbyter placing his hands in the hands of the bishop. However, the major novelty here is that the directives allow for episcopal conferences to choose another form:[43]

"Then the candidate goes to the bishop and, kneeling before him, places his joined hands between those of the bishop. If this gesture seems less suitable in some places, the conference of bishops may choose another gesture or sign."[44]

This simply affirms the historical context of the joining of the hands, a context that is not intrinsic to orders or obedience. It would seem that the door is open for further study of rituals of obedience, especially in the context of cultural adaptation.

Finally, we need to ask about the novelty of a promise of obedience in the rite of ordination of deacons. This is the first time such a promise appears. The rationale seems to be that the promise of obedience is part of the rite of ordination of deacons because it is now an order unto itself and no longer simply a step toward the presbyterate, and it is needed to remind the candidate that he is ordained for service to the Church under obedience to the bishop.[45] Likewise, this is part of the ancient tradition of deacons being attached to the order of

[41] *De Ordinatione Diaconi, Presbyteri et Episcopi,* no. 16 for both deacons and presbyters. English translation from *The Roman Pontifical,* International Commission on English in the Liturgy, 1978.

[42] Andrieu, *Le Pontifical Romain,* 3:372. *Pontificale Romanum,* 57–8.

[43] Kleinheyer, "L'Ordination de Prêtres," 109.

[44] *De Ordinatione,* no. 16 for both deacons and priests.

[45] Kleinheyer, "Ordinationen und Beauftragungen," 49.

bishops.[46] However, to ensure a broader understanding of their ministry, deacons are asked in their *examinatio* if they accept their office to assist the bishop and the priests.

One element that will help shed light on both the intentionality and repetition of these promises of obedience is the profession of faith that had been demanded of candidates for major orders since Trent and was expressed by Canon 1406 of the 1917 Code of Canon Law.[47] Beginning with the subdiaconate and repeated each time a candidate petitioned for orders, he was required to submit a written profession of faith to his ordinary, using a formula approved by the Holy See. The text of Canon 1406 gives a rather broad purpose for this profession, especially section 7, which highlights the concern for believing and teaching sound doctrine:

"The following must make profession before the local ordinary or his delegate: (a) the vicar general; (b) pastors and those provided with a benefice (even though manual only) to which the care of souls is attached; (c) rectors of seminaries and professors of sacred theology, canon law, and philosophy, at the beginning of each scholastic year, or at least when they assume office; (d) those about to be ordained subdeacons; (e) the censors of books, as mentioned in can. 1393; (f) all priests who are to act as confessors or preachers, before they are given their appointment or faculties. Under this heading, no doubt, also come our assistants or curates, and the confessors and chaplains of nuns and religious institutions."[48]

This profession of faith taken by subdeacons, deacons, and presbyters, while varied and changing over the centuries, is basically a development of the oaths taken by bishops to the pope over the centuries. In the centuries after Trent such an oath was demanded of all petitioning for orders. Here is the version from 1930 that was in use until after the revisions of the Second Vatican Council, when a new oath was drawn up in 1967.[49]

---

[46] Cnudde, "L'Ordination des Diacres," 86.

[47] Nabuco, *Pontificalis Romani,* 1:69–71.

[48] Augustine, *Commentary on the New Code of Canon Law,* 6:485–9, text and commentary.

[49] For a short history see Betti, "Professio Fidei" et "Iusiurandum Fidelitatis," 319–25.

"I, the undersigned N. N., in presenting to the Bishop my petition for the reception of the subdiaconate (or the diaconate or the presbyterate), as the time for the sacred ordination is near at hand, having carefully considered the matter before God *(coram Deo)*, do upon my oath *(iuramento interposito)* testify in the first place that I am urged by no sort of compulsion or force or fear in receiving the aforesaid sacred order, but that I do spontaneously desire and of my own full and free will wish to receive the same, because I know and feel that I am truly called by God. I acknowledge that I know fully all the burdens and other consequences which flow from the said sacred order, and these I freely wish and propose to assume; and with the grace of God I resolve to keep them most faithfully during my whole life.

"I declare especially that I am clearly aware of what the law of celibacy entails; and I firmly resolve with the help of God to fulfill that law willingly and to keep it in its entirety until the end.

"Finally, I sincerely promise *(sincera fide spondeo)* that I shall always, according to the sacred canons, obey most exactly *(obtemperaturum obsequentissime)* all the precepts of my Superiors and whatever the discipline of the Church requires, being prepared to give an example of virtue either in work or in word, in suchwise that I may deserve to be rewarded by God for the assumption of so great an office.

"This I promise, this I vow, this I swear, so help me God and these sacred Gospels which I touch with my hand. *(Sic spondeo, sic voveo, sic juro, sic me Deus adjuvet et haec Sancta Dei Evangelia, Quae manibus meis tango.)*"[50]

This is more an oath of fidelity than a profession of faith, and its major concern is loyalty to the discipline and laws of the Church. The use of "I promise," "an oath," and "I swear" all point to the vocabulary of oaths we have studied. Second, it is concerned that the candidate make this promise freely, another common element of these oaths. Third, while there is no mention of obedience to either the bishop or the pope, obedience to the canons of church law is demanded "most exactly." Celibacy is mentioned in particular, implying

---

[50] *Acta Apostolicae Sedis* 23 (1931) 127. Commentary in Woywod, *Practical Commentary on the Code of Canon Law,* 671–3. English translation: Bouscaren, *Canon Law Digest,* 471–2.

that this promise required some special attention. Finally, this promise takes on some of the elements of the petitions that were a part of religious professions. It is a written document that is signed, and it is professed with one's hands on the Gospels. While it is directed to a person in authority, the promise is made before God. We also find the use of "I vow," which is part of the vocabulary of religious vows. Thus it seems this profession was influenced by some of the elements of religious rites of profession.

With the publication of the typical edition with the rites of ordination in 1968, the whole issue of minor orders was left in limbo.[51] Since the promise of obedience was now included in the rite of ordination of deacons, the major issue became the place and shape of the promise of celibacy. With the proposed suppression of the subdiaconate, the rite of ordination to the diaconate became the prime time for the issues of loyalty to the Church and obedience to its laws. What is curious is that the promise of celibacy was not part of the 1968 typical edition for the ordination of deacons. It did not become a part of the rite until after the 1972 motu proprio *Ad pascendum*,[52] in which Paul VI laid down certain norms regarding the order of deacons. Still, there was much discussion concerning how this promise of celibacy should be ritualized.[53] Canonically, this was not a pressing issue at the time because candidates for the diaconate still took and signed the profession of faith before ordination to the diaconate, a profession of faith that included a promise of celibacy.[54] However, there was a desire to excise from the rites of ordination those elements that reflected the mentality and spirituality of another time, such as the taking of an oath of fidelity, an in-

---

[51] See Bugnini, *Reform of the Liturgy*, 727–51.

[52] *Acta Apostolicae Sedis* 64, (1972) 534–40. Here is the significant text: "Candidati ad Diaconatum, ante ordinationem, Ordinario (Episcopo et, in clericalibus institutis perfectionis, Superiori Maiori) tradant declarationem propria manu exaratam et subscriptam, qua testificentur se sponte ac libere sacrum ordinem suscepturos esse.

"Consecratio propria caelibatus, propter Regnum caelorum servati, huiusque obligatio pro candidatis ad Sacerdotium et pro candidatis non uxoratis ad Diaconatum reapse connectuntur cum Diaconatu. Publica ipsius sacri caelibatus assumptio coram Deo et Ecclesia etiam a religiosis celebranda est speciali ritu, qui ordinationem diaconalem praecedat."

[53] Bugnini, *Reform of the Liturgy*, 749–51.

[54] However, this promise of celibacy still had to be based on the 1930 profession of faith since the new profession of faith of 1967 no longer contained such a promise. *Acta Apostolicae Sedis* 59 (1967) 1058.

fluence of feudalism.[55] Thus we have the movement from an oath of fidelity, or "profession of faith," as it was called, taken in a private ceremony the night before, to a public commitment done in the context of the rite of ordination itself. We must ask if we really have succeeded in capturing the desire of the council to arrive at a more mature sign and celebration of the promises of celibacy and obedience.

Finally we have the question of repetition. The promise of obedience to the bishop is a part of the 1968 typical edition of the rite of ordination for the diaconate, and it is repeated again for the presbyterate. The reason for the repetition is that the presbyterate is another order. What is curious is that the promise of celibacy is not repeated, especially since one of the focuses of the repeated profession of faith was celibacy. Likewise, this is curious since promises of both celibacy and obedience will be part of the renewal of priestly promises in the revised Chrism Mass. This question is one yet to be studied and resolved.

Now we turn to the rite of ordination of bishops. As we noted in the discussion of the revised rites of ordination of presbyters and deacons, the *examinatio* is now a part of the rite of ordination itself. It is no longer an extrinsic ritual that could be done at some other time, as in the Tridentine rite. This is happily part of the desire to make such questioning public in order that it might carry a proper solemnity,[56] and there is a new series of questions designed to highlight the pastoral role of the bishop.[57] The present rite has two questions that contain promises of obedience to the pope as successor of Peter. However, the initial schema for the revised rite of ordination of bishops contained only the first of these two questions.[58] This first statement has a theological base, the building up of the Church, is well written, and seems to flow from the teachings of the Second Vatican Council, even capturing the proper tension the council documents maintained:[59]

[55] Bugnini, *Reform of the Liturgy*, 708.

[56] Ibid., 719.

[57] B. Botte, "L'Ordination de L'Évêque," 117.

[58] Bugnini, *Reform of the Liturgy*, 711–2; Botte, "L'Ordination de L'Évêque," 117–8.

[59] The wording of this question reflects *Lumen Gentium* 27 and *Christus Dominus* 1 and 3, where bishops are to make use of their power for the building up of the Church ("ad gregem suum in veritate et sanctitate aedificandum utuntur," *LG* 27),

"Are you resolved *(Vis)* to build up the Church as the body of Christ and to remain united to it within the order of bishops under the authority of the successor of the apostle Peter *(in eius unitate cum ordine Episcoporum, sub auctoritate successoris beati Petri Apostoli)? I am. (Volo)."*[60]

However, in a letter from the Congregation of the Faith dated November 8, 1967, the Congregation, while approving the new schema, made several qualifications. It expressly asked:

"In the questions asked of the candidate for the episcopal office, greater emphasis should be put on faith and its conscientious transmission; moreover, the candidate should be expressly asked about his determination to give obedience to the Roman Pontiff."[61]

This resulted in the second question concerning obedience to the pope being added:

"Are you resolved to be faithful in your obedience to the successor of the apostle Peter *(Vis beati Petri Apostoli successori oboedientiam fideliter exhibere)? I am. (Volo)."*[62]

First, the question is very short and succinct. The use of "successor of Peter" is faithful to the traditional usage found in previous rites of ordination of bishops and a far more theological term than "Roman pontiff." Second, the elect is asked to be obedient to the successor of Peter, without any further ecclesial or theological context. Finally, the use of "to faithfully exhibit," or as our English texts translate it, "resolved to be faithful," follows the terminology of the blessing of abbots more than that of the consecration of bishops in the Tridentine rite.[63] The problem is that this second question asking obedience to the pope seems to add nothing to what is included in the first question.[64]

---

because as successors of the apostles they were sent "in aedificationem Corporis Christi *(Eph* 4,12) quod est Ecclesia" *(CD* 1). They must do their office "sub auctoritate Summi Pontificis exercent, ad magisterium et regimen pastorale quod attinet, omnes uniti in Collegio seu corpore quoad universam Dei Ecclesiam" *(CD* 3).

[60] *De Ordinatione,* no. 19.
[61] English translation in Bugnini, *Reform of the Liturgy,* 712.
[62] *De Ordinatione,* no. 19.
[63] *Pontificale Romanum,* 64–5, 101–2.
[64] Botte, "L'Ordination de L'Évêque," 118.

In summation, we have a new role for the *examinatio* in all three rites of ordination. The *examinatio* is to give solemnity to the public commitment of those seeking orders while also accenting the reciprocal nature of the responsibility of both parties. All three *examinationes* have promises of obedience. This is part of the tendency toward ritual and theological symmetry, as now all three rites have similar structures. Thus, the promise of obedience for deacons is new. What is given a secondary role is the joining of the hands, which can be replaced with another ritual action if the episcopal conference so decides.

Some of the issues not resolved include the relationship between deacons and presbyters. The deacon is ordained to ministry in obedience to the bishop and to be of help to the presbyters. The presbyter is ordained to the priesthood of Christ in obedience to and in union with the bishop. Second, the full implications of the movement from the profession of faith or oath of fidelity taken and signed before ordination to the *examinatio* professed during the rite itself have not been thought through. The traditional profession of faith was far more a general commitment to the laws and teachings of the Church, which in particular included celibacy, than the more personal promise of obedience made to the local bishop. This is the same movement evident in the historical development of rites of profession of religious. We must ask if this is needed for the good of order and ministry in the Church of our day. In particular, we must ask if the second specific promise of obedience of bishops to the pope is really necessary. Third, we have the issue of repetition. Why do presbyters repeat the same promise of obedience they made at their diaconate ordination? Why not then repeat the promise of celibacy? What about the renewal of these promises? To shed more light on this issue we now turn to the revision of the Chrism Mass with its renewal of priestly promises.

RENEWAL OF COMMITMENT TO PRIESTLY SERVICE IN THE CHRISM MASS

The rationale for the study of this particular issue is simple. First, these texts deal with the renewal of the very promises made at ordination. Second, the development of these texts and this ceremony is contemporary with the revision of the rites of ordination, namely 1969, and thus will shed further light on the thinking of the time. Finally, the issues of the repetition of promises can now also be seen in the context of their renewal.

The concept of transforming the Chrism Mass into a feast of the priesthood came from Pope Paul VI, who did such a transformation in Milan. Very simply, the historical development of the Chrism Mass is as follows. When the Holy Thursday evening Mass, the Mass of the Lord's Supper, was transferred to the morning in the Middle Ages, its themes were amalgamated with the themes of the Chrism Mass. Thus, we have the beginnings of the mixture of the themes of the holy oils with the Eucharist and priesthood. With the Holy Week reforms of 1955, these two masses and their respective themes were separated again. However, with the return of concelebration at the Chrism Mass and the long history of its connection to the Eucharist and priesthood, even though some liturgists were opposed to this mixing of purposes, the renewal of priestly promises at the Chrism Mass became part of the revision.[65]

The actual impetus for this development began with a circular letter from the Sacred Congregation for the Clergy on November 4, 1969, signed by Cardinal John Wright. Section 9 calls for the renewal of priestly promises and puts it in its context:

"By divine institution, the Supreme Shepherd of the Church and the bishops in conjunction with him have the duty of teaching those things that relate to the faith. This power does not reside with lay people or priests. So what the magisterium propounds must be accepted wholeheartedly. All its pronouncements must be accepted without reservation or doubt; otherwise everything becomes vain and useless. Because of the help of the Holy Spirit that was promised to the Church's magisterium, taking for granted all that has to be taken for granted *(suppositis quidem supponendis)*, 'religious assent of intellect and will *(religiosum voluntatis et intellectus obsequium)* must be accorded in a special way to the authentic teaching authority of the Roman Pontiff, even when he is not speaking *ex cathedra,*' and to definitions of the supreme mageristerium, 'which must be accepted as matters of faith' *(LG* 25).

"To reinforce the awareness and spiritual life of the priest *(sacerdotii)*, it is hoped that on Holy Thursday morning every priest *(presbyter)*, whether he attends the Mass of the Chrism or not, would renew the act of dedication to Christ *(renovet actum quo se Christo devovit)* in

[65] Bugnini, *Reform of the Liturgy,* 116–7. Russo, "La MISSA CRISMAL," 201–29.

which he promised to carry out his priestly functions and, in particular, to preserve holy celibacy and to obey his bishop *(oboedientiam
Episcopo)* or religious superior. It is hoped that he will commemorate
the solemn obligation he undertook at ordination, when he was called
into the service of the church."[66]

What is immediately obvious is that the major concern here is the
teaching of orthodox theology and doctrines approved by the magisterium. This context is therefore very similar to the profession of faith
demanded of all seeking major orders by the 1917 Code of Canon
Law. The quoting of *Lumen Gentium* 25, with its call for the submission of the will and intellect, places the revision of the Chrism Mass
with its renewal of priestly promises in a very particular context, such
that obedience and celibacy are seen in the singular context of faith-
fulness to the teachings of the Church. It is implied that if one is faithful to the teachings of the Church, he will also be faithful to his
promise of celibacy and obedience to his bishop or religious superior.
Completely lacking is any notion of the corporate image of the presbyterium or any notion of reciprocity between presbyter and bishop.
Likewise there is no sense of the maturity demanded of a promise of
obedience as taught by the council. The context is a very narrow desire for doctrinal fidelity, one that is rather negative in style, demanding assent without any thought of dialogue.

The Congregation of Divine Worship then prepared such a renewal
of priestly promises and published them on March 6, 1970. In its introduction to the texts themselves it gives some of the history of this
development and then, in speaking of the renewal of promises themselves, states that just as religious renew their vows of profession, so it
is proper that priests should renew the promises they made to the
bishop on the day of their ordination.[67] Here again we have an influence from religious life. Here are those texts:

"My brothers, today we celebrate the memory of the first eucharist, at
which our Lord Jesus Christ shared with his apostles and with us his
call to the priestly service of his Church *(sacerdotium cum Apostolis*

---

[66] *Acta Apostolicae Sedis* 62 (1970) 126–7. English translation: *The Pope Speaks* 15
(1970) 75–83.
[67] Text found in *Notitiae* 6 (1970) 87–9.

nobisque communicavit). Now, in the presence of your bishop and God's holy people, are you ready to renew your own dedication to Christ as priests of his new covenant *(vultis olim factas promissiones coram Episcopo vestro et populo sancto Dei renovare)?* I am. *(Volo).*

"At your ordination you accepted the responsibilities of the priest-hood out of love for the Lord Jesus and his Church. Are you resolved *(Vultis)* to unite yourselves more closely to Christ and to try to become more like him by joyfully sacrificing your own pleasure and ambition to bring his peace and love to your brothers and sisters? I am. *(Volo).*

"Are you resolved *(Vultis)* to be faithful ministers of the mysteries of God, to celebrate the eucharist and the other liturgical services with sincere devotion? Are you resolved to imitate Jesus Christ, the head and shepherd of the Church, by teaching the Christian faith without thinking of your own profit, solely for the well-being of the people you were sent to serve? I am. *(Volo).*"[68]

What is most curious is that the promises of obedience and celibacy are not mentioned in particular, especially since the letter from the Congregation for Clergy expressly called for this. Rather, we have a general renewal of promises more akin to a renewal of a religious profession than of the specific promises made at ordination. Second, these promises lack much of the development of the teachings of the council on the presbyterate.[69] The first question lacks completely the central idea of presbyters as cooperators with the order of bishops. The second question, drawing from language found in rites of religious profession, gives a very negative and ascetic image of following Christ in ministry. The third question speaks of the ministerial functions of the presbyter but without any reference to the plurality of ministry in the Church. It seems that a great opportunity for a fuller vision of renewal of priestly promises was missed.

Likewise there are other issues, such as the wisdom of the placement of such a renewal in the context of the Chrism Mass. These two celebrations, each with important purposes, do not flow well together.[70]

[68] *Missale Romanum,* Editio Typica Altera, 1975.
[69] Russo, "La MISSA CRISMAL," 221.
[70] Kleinheyer, "Chrismamesse oder Erneuerung der priesterlichen Versprechen?" 16–7. Russo, "La MISSA CRISMAL," 222.

Finally, we must ask the rationale behind this development of the renewal of priestly promises in the Chrism Mass. It can only be understood in the political situation of the great exodus of presbyters shortly after the council.[71] This appears an attempt to renew the priesthood in a public manner to help those still faithful in the ministry to remain there. It would seem a rather blatant example of the desire to respond to a political situation with external celebrations in which neither ecclesial tradition nor conciliar theology are well served.

In summation, the renewal of priestly promises as part of the Chrism Mass should be understood in the political situation of the exodus of presbyters shortly after the council. It is an attempt to help form obedient presbyters by the public renewal of these promises. Thus this ritual has a very narrow design, and unfortunately the texts show a rather meager use of the richness of the theological developments of the council on the priesthood. Prescinding from when and where such a ritual should be celebrated, a great opportunity for a positive celebration of the renewal of priestly service in the Church was missed.

The history of the development of this ritual sheds some light on the development of the rites of ordination and both the additions of and struggles with promises of obedience and celibacy. It points to the struggle between those dedicated to the study of rituals of ordination and those concerned with the present state of affairs in the priesthood. While this struggle can bear fruit, it often results in compromises that do justice to neither. There is need for a continual reform of the rituals that celebrate the life of the Church.

ECCLESIOLOGICAL REFLECTIONS

We must acknowledge the richness of the theological developments of the Second Vatican Council and, in particular, the return to an understanding of bishops as possessing the fullness of the priesthood and of presbyters as united with their bishops in that one priesthood of Christ. The council advanced the understanding of obedience as leading to the full maturity of sons and daughters of God. This concept is reflected in the revised rites of ordination in the new *examinationes,* which enhance the reciprocal aspects of the relationships involved in the reception of orders. The promise of obedience for a

[71] Kleinheyer, "Chrismamesse," 17.

deacon, presbyter, or bishop is proclaimed in a public, solemn manner. All three rites are similar in structure, reflecting the desire for ritual and theological symmetry.

Some of the issues of these developments that need further clarification are the fuller implications of the relationships between deacons and presbyters, religious and diocesan presbyters, and bishops and the pope. In the relationship between presbyter and bishop, how the scholastic concept of order and jurisdiction is to be understood in our day still needs to be clarified.

Concerning the role of the promise of obedience in the rites of ordination, there is need to clarify the relationship between the profession of faith, or oath of fidelity, which was directed at obedience to the teachings and disciplines of the Church, and the continued use of a promise of obedience to the person of the bishop or pope. Here we add the issues of the repetition of such promises and the issues of the renewal of such promises in the Chrism Mass. It would seem that further reflection on the understanding that obedience flows out of and leads to maturity is needed. It would also seem that external rituals in which such promises are first made and then repeated or renewed depend on the free will of the subjects of the ritual. This returns us to one of the major elements of oaths of fidelity, namely, that the person knowingly and freely make such promises. It would seem that only a priestly formation that leads to such maturity can be worthily celebrated in such rituals.

Further reflection on the living out of obedience seems to indicate that there are only two reasons to carry out the decisions of a superior. Very simply, these are the willingness of the person to fulfill that decision because he is open to it or the decision makes sense to him or, secondarily, because of respect for his superior. When a presbyter is willing to take an assignment or leave one, or when he is open to new challenges or willing to leave a good situation to take on a new task because of the needs of the people, there is much good will in accepting the decision of the bishop or superior. If the presbyter is not ready for a new assignment, or is very happy where he is, or perhaps is too content and not ready for new and radical changes in his life, the superior will need to speak to the logic of the good of the decision and hope that this will convince the presbyter of its wisdom both for his ministry and for that of the Church. If logic and reason do not move the presbyter to a willingness to comply with the decision, then the superior has only one option. He must ask the presbyter to trust in the presence of the Holy Spirit to lead and guide the Church and her ministers through his ministry. If the presbyter and superior have a relationship based on trust and respect, and if both have a healthy human formation and a ministerial formation based on the gospels, then the superior can ask the presbyter to accept his decision out of respect for not only his office but also his person. This is the key. Too often presbyters are asked to accept difficult decisions because of the office of bishop or superior and not because of respect for the person who holds that office. A bishop or superior must treasure the respect of those entrusted to him and, through a shared vision based on gospel values and out of a lived spirituality based on those values, must lead his priests to carry out the mission of Jesus and his Church. Any decision not arrived at with these conditions is abusive. The need for a priestly formation based on such maturity is essential.

A deeper reflection on the mysteries of God's call to ministry in the Church, and the caution that God wishes the full mystery of the person to be developed, are necessary if the true building up of the Church is to take place. These are issues with which the Church, *semper reformanda*, continues to struggle.

5

The Revisions of 1990

First of all, there are changes in the title, *The Ordination of a Bishop, of Presbyters, and of Deacons*. While this inversion was not completely novel,[1] it represents far more than just a cosmetic change. The title now reflects the theological realities dictated by the teachings of the Second Vatican Council, that of the episcopacy as the fullness of orders, and more importantly, that of the presbyterate and diaconate as sharing in those orders.[2] Thus it makes theological sense for the ordination of a bishop to be first. Likewise, the use of the singular reflects the unitive function of the one who serves in the place of the apostles. The rites of ordination for presbyters and deacons follow, both in the plural, reflecting the theological reality of an order of presbyters and deacons surrounding the local bishop.

Moreover, there are some significant changes in the rites themselves.[3] First, there is an introduction, or *praenotanda*. This is new, as there was none in the 1968 edition. Second, the prayers of ordination for both presbyters and deacons have been expanded and modified to better express both the nature and the function of these orders. Third, the reference to the power of the forgiveness of sins, a large part of the Tridentine rite and not mentioned in the 1968 edition, has been added to the examination for presbyters. Fourth, the promise of celibacy for deacons, not included in the 1968 edition but mandated by *Ad pascendum* in 1972 and added in the various vernacular editions, is now a part of the Latin text. Finally, and most significant, members of institutes

---

[1] Both the French and Italian language editions of the 1968 rite had inverted both the order and the title. Kleinheyer, "Ordinationsfeiern," 91.

[2] Lessi-Ariosto, "Commentarium," 96.

[3] "Decretum," *De Ordinatione Episcopi, Presbyterorum et Diaconorum.*

of consecrated life are now asked to make a promise of obedience and respect to the local diocesan bishop as well as to their own superiors in the rites of ordination to both the diaconate and presbyterate.

THE GENERAL INTRODUCTION
(*PRAENOTANDA GENERALIA*)

The Introduction, or *Praenotanda*, is a work that had been in process since 1974.[4] What is of interest is the theological descriptions employed for bishop, presbyter, and deacon. Bishops are described as having the fullness of orders, a quote from *Lumen Gentium* 26, and then they are further called true and authentic teachers of the faith, pontiffs and pastors, a quote from *Christus Dominus* 2.[5] It would seem that in its simplicity this statement has maintained the dignity and authority of each bishop.

For presbyters the introduction simply quotes *Lumen Gentium* 28, in which presbyters are seen as joined in the honor of the priesthood with their bishops, but the exercise of their power is dependent on the bishops.[6] What is unfortunate is that the strong image of presbyters as co-operators with the bishops, an image also found in *Lumen Gentium* 28, is not included here. We have to wait until the introduction proper to the ordination of presbyters to find this image.[7] It would seem that the image of cooperators with the bishops is a concept more central to the theology of presbyters and might have served its purpose better there.

For deacons we have a summary of *Lumen Gentium* 29, in which deacons are seen as ordained for ministry and not for priesthood, but in communion with their bishop they are to be of service to the presbyterate as well.[8] There seems to be no further development in the theology of the diaconate and how it relates to the presbyterate.

The third section of the general *praenotanda* covers the various adaptations available to episcopal conferences.[9] This is an important part of the inculturation of the Roman Rite in the various cultures and

---

[4] Dell'Oro, "La 'Editio typica altera' del Pontificale Romano delle Ordinazione," 287–92.

[5] *De Ordinatione Episcopi, Presbyterorum et Diaconorum*, no. 3.

[6] Ibid., no. 4.

[7] Ibid., no. 101.

[8] Ibid., no. 5.

[9] Ibid., no. 11.

languages of the world. The first adaptation concerns the assent of the community to the election of the candidate for orders and the form this may take. It is unfortunate that this important element has been given very little development, both in its theological ramifications and in its ritual expression. It would seem that a greater acknowledgment of the role of the community in both the call and the formation of the person being ordained is needed.

Second, if opportune further questions may be added to the *examinatio*. This allows for the public interrogation of a candidate's suitability for orders to be determined by the needs of the local community. Again, the ritual implications of such a theological and cultural adaptation need further development.

Third, and most important, the form by which candidates for the diaconate and presbyterate promise obedience can be defined by local episcopal conferences. As in the 1968 typical edition, this seems to refer more to the ritual gestures that accompany the words of the promise of obedience than to the actual words themselves. While this allows for the traditional joining of the hands to be replaced by some other gesture, it would seem that there are other questions, both cultural and theological, that would shape how a local church ritualizes obedience. For example, a more personal *promitto* statement, read by the candidate and well written to avoid superficiality, could serve the ritual necessities of a promise of obedience in many cultures. The actual wording could reflect a better ecclesial connection. Some mention of the local diocese would serve well here. These ritual possibilities have precedents, as chapter 2 has shown. The Church shapes both the form and the wording to meet the needs of the local church. It seems more possibilities could have been allowed here.

Now returning to our list of possible adaptations, the fourth part concerns the expression of the promise of celibacy. Here the possibilities for adaptation seem to be broader, "that the responsibility of assuming of the obligation of celibacy . . . may be manifested by some external formula." While again there is precedent for this promise to take many different verbal forms, it is curious that there are more possibilities for the adaptation of the promise of celibacy than for the promise of obedience. Both the promise of celibacy and the promise of obedience have a long theological and ritual history in the life of the Church for those being ordained for ministry. It would seem that more flexibility for both promises would be advantageous for the cultural adaptation of the rites of ordination.

The fifth area for adaptation concerns the use of hymns in the rites themselves.

The sixth and final area for adaptation is the general norm that episcopal conferences can propose other adaptations to the Apostolic See. However, the laying on of hands can never be omitted and the ordination prayer may not be shortened nor may it be replaced with another prayer. Simply put, the general structure and nature of the rite and its various elements are to be respected. This allows for the various episcopal conferences and the episcopal committees responsible for the various language groups to take a serious look at both the form and the wording of the promise of obedience as they prepare the texts of the second typical edition for use in their countries. With this work in mind, we turn to the texts themselves.

THE PROMISE OF OBEDIENCE FOR RELIGIOUS TO THE DIOCESAN BISHOP IN THE RITES OF ORDINATION OF PRESBYTERS AND DEACONS

While there are revisions in the rite for the ordination of a bishop, there are none that concern the promise of obedience of bishops to the pope. Therefore, we begin with the rites of ordination of presbyters and deacons.

The major revision, and one with significant theological ramifications, is the addition of a promise of obedience for religious to the local diocesan bishop in the rites of ordination of both presbyters and of deacons. Since the wording for the promises of obedience for both orders is exactly the same,[10] we can treat them together.

"The bishop questions the elect, saying, if he is his Ordinary: Do you promise me and my successors respect and obedience *(Promittis mihi et successoribus meis reverentiam et oboedientiam)?* I promise *(Promitto).*

"If the bishop is not his Ordinary, he says: Do you promise respect and obedience to your Ordinary *(Promittis Ordinario tuo reverentiam et oboedientiam)?* I promise *(Promitto).*

"If the elect is a religious, the bishop says: Do you promise the diocesan Bishop and also your legitimate Superior respect and obedience

[10] Ibid., no. 125 and no. 201.

110

(Promittis Episcopo diocesano necnon legitimo Superiori tuo reverentiam et oboedientiam)? I promise *(Promitto)."*

There are two major issues involved here. The first concerns the addition of the special promise of obedience to the local diocesan bishop for religious. The second concerns the repetition of the same promise of obedience in both the rite of ordination to the diaconate and the rite of ordination to the presbyterate.

To understand the development of this rite, we turn to the work of the committee Concerning holy Orders, which began its final and decisive phase in 1985 under the leadership of professor Reiner Kaczynski.[11] The work of this committee was discussed by the members and consultors of the Congregation of Divine Worship on May 20–24, 1985, with the result that their schemas, to date, were approved with some modifications.[12] The committee then proceeded with its work, part of which is the following schema, from July 9, 1985, which contains a new wording of the promise of obedience for presbyters. The significance is that this formula is different from the one used for deacons. The formula for deacons would remain the same as the one in the 1968 typical edition. Here is the formula for a presbyter:[13]

"The bishop questions the elect, saying, if he is his Ordinary: Do you promise me and my successors as a member of the presbyterate of the Church of N. respect and obedience *(Promittis mihi et successoribus meis tamquam membrum presbyterii Ecclesiae N. reverentiam et oboedientiam)?* I promise *(Promitto).*

"If the bishop is not his Ordinary, he says: Do you promise your Ordinary as a member of the presbyterate of the Church of N. respect and obedience *(Promittis Ordinario tuo tamquam membrum presbyterii Ecclesiae N. reverentiam et oboedientiam)?* I promise *(Promitto).*

"If the elect is a religious, the bishop says: Do you promise your Ordinary respect and obedience *(Promittis Ordinario tuo reverentiam et oboedientiam)?* I promise *(Promitto)."*

---

[11] Dell'Oro, "La 'Editio typica altera'" 296–300.
[12] *Notitiae* 21 (1985) 379.
[13] From personal correspondence with Prof. Reiner Kaczynski.

The major change is the addition for diocesan presbyters of the concept of an order of presbyters of a particular diocese. The elect is asked to promise obedience to his bishop as a member of the presbyterate of his particular diocese. Also, the naming of the diocese is a good ecclesiological statement. The wording for religious presbyters was not changed from the 1968 typical edition.

The work of this committee was further discussed in the plenary session of the Congregation of Divine Worship on October 15–16, 1985.[14] Both questions, the one concerning a different formula for the promise of obedience for presbyters than for deacons, and the one concerning the promise of obedience for religious presbyters, were discussed, but for both the results remained inconclusive.[15]

These questions, among others, were sent to the secretary of the Congregation of the Doctrine of the Faith by Archbishop Noé on May 20, 1986:[16]

"Concerning the wording for the promise of obedience for presbyters, there still remains some problems to be solved. What is the thinking of this Congregation:

a) regarding the desire of various Fathers that religious priests should make a promise of obedience to the diocesan bishop;

b) regarding the acceptance of the text formulated in the schema (the new one above);

c) regarding the keeping of the text from the typical edition of 1968, now in use, for both presbyters as well as deacons."

The first issue concerned religious presbyters. We are told that various Fathers wanted religious presbyters to make a promise of obedience to the diocesan bishop. This became part of the second typical edition. Since this is a new development, its implications will take generations to comprehend. The second issue concerned the acceptance of different formulas of obedience for presbyters than for deacons. Unfortunately this was not accepted, and the same formulas from the 1968 typical edition for both presbyter and deacon remain, which answered the third issue.

[14] *Notitiae* 21 (1985) 579.
[15] From personal correspondence with Prof. Kaczynski.
[16] Ibid. (Text from Prot. 622/86).

With these issues resolved the schemas were approved by the plenary session of the Congregation for Divine Worship on May 21, 1987,[17] and sent on to the Congregation for the Doctrine of the Faith for their approval. Likewise these schemas were sent to the Secretariat of State.

During the plenary session of the Congregation for Divine Worship, November 29–December 3, 1988, it was reported that the final redaction of *Concerning holy Orders* was prepared. With the final approval of the Congregation of the Doctrine of the Faith, it had gone to the Pope at the end of June.[18] However, they had not yet received a response from the Secretariat of State.

The text for the second typical edition received its final approval from the Pope on May 10, 1989.[19] The Decree of the Congregation of Divine Worship, which promulgated the text, was dated June 29, 1989. Its actual publication date was May 31, 1990.[20]

Now we return to the issue of the wording of the promise of obedience for both deacons and presbyters being exactly the same. While the ecclesial reality of obedience is the same for deacons and presbyters, as both are subject to the local bishop, the theological reality of these two orders is quite distinct. The council documents and the explanatory texts of both the typical edition and second typical edition are careful to state that presbyters share in the priesthood of their bishops while deacons are ordained for ministry and not to priesthood. It would likewise seem that the ritual expression of obedience should be distinct for these two orders. Thus further study of the implications of this theological distinction and its possible expression in a ritual promise of obedience would be advantageous. The proposed schema of the committee Concerning holy Orders, which we studied above, attempted to answer this distinction. While this proposal was

---

[17] *Notitiae* 23 (1987) 1020, "Si spera di giungere entro breve tempo alla redazione finalle della editio typica altera, dopo le osservazioni pervenute dalla Congregazione per la Dottrina della Fede, per poi presentarla alla definitiva approvazione del Santo Padre."

[18] *Notitiae* 25 (1988) 35. "La redazione finale è stata preparata, si ha già avuto il beneplacito della Congregazione per la Dottrina della Fede. È stata mandata a suo tempo, a fine giugno, al Santo Padre direttamente, ma fino a questo momento dalla Segreteria di Stato non si è avuto alcuna risposta."

[19] *Notititae* 26 (1990) 95.

[20] Dell'Oro, "La 'Editio typica altera,'" 300.

not accepted, the norms of adaptation presented in the introduction would allow for such a distinction in wording.[21] The possibility of an ecclesially or theologically richer wording of the promise of obedience for presbyters than for deacons would seem worthy of study by the various language groups and episcopal conferences as they prepare their vernacular texts.

Second, concerning the special promise of obedience for both religious deacons and presbyters to the local diocesan bishop, we can make some general observations, raise some specific issues that are not yet resolved, and attempt to project into the future some of the implications not yet seen with this addition.

In general, the promise of obedience of religious, both deacons and presbyters, to the local diocesan bishop flows out of the basic teachings of *Christus Dominus* 35. Numbers 1 and 4, which we studied in chapter 4, and the August 6, 1966, apostolic letter on the implementation of the decrees *Christus Dominus, Presbyterorum Ordinis,* and *Perfectae Caritatis (Ecclesiae Sanctae)* 22–26,[22] both of which emphasize the need for harmony in the pastoral ministry of a diocese.[23] Both state that religious are subject to the local bishop in all aspects of their public ministry and worship. This same basic understanding of the relationship between the pastoral ministry of religious and the local bishop was codified in the 1983 Code of Canon Law in Canons 678 and 681. It seems that this special promise of obedience made by religious to the local diocesan bishop developed out of an ecclesiological understanding of the diocese as the local church, and thus the need for the unity of all pastoral ministry in that diocese under the authority of the local bishop.

In terms of the diocesan presbyterate gathered around and sharing in the priesthood of their bishop, it makes perfect sense to speak of this unity of priestly service. In terms of religious presbyters sharing in this same theological image, the fuller implications are yet to be resolved. However, it seems that since religious presbyters likewise

<hr>

[21] Kaczynski, "Ein neues Pontifikale für die katholischen Bistümer des deutschen Sprachgebietes," 239.

[22] *Acta Apostolicae Sedis* 58 (1966) 769–70. English translation in A. Flannery, *Vatican Council II: The Conciliar and Post Conciliar Documents,* 1988 revised edition, 604–5.

[23] P. Jounel, "La Nouvelle Édition Typique du Rituel des Ordinations," 11; Kleinheyer, "Ordinationsfeiern," 113-4.

share in the one priesthood of Christ, which the bishops possess in its fullness, this unity of priesthood is realized in the life of the local diocesan church under the authority of the local bishop. Thus, it seems that this special promise of obedience for religious to the local bishop makes a significant theological statement. It seems to further clarify that the exercise of priestly ministry of religious presbyters is not only dependent on its sharing the one priesthood of Christ, which the bishops have in its fullness as we read in *Lumen Gentium* 28, but more specifically, it is dependent on the power and authority of the singular, local diocesan bishop. This seems to be confirmed in the wording of *Christus Dominus* 28, where it states that both diocesan and religious presbyters "share and exercise the one priesthood of Christ with the bishop." Thus it seems that this ritual addition is an important element in the development of the ecclesiology of how diocesan and religious presbyters relate to each other and to the local bishop and, in fact, seems to be a logical development.

This development seems to have been confirmed in the 1992 papal exhortation, "I Will Give You Shepherds" *(Pastores Dabo Vobis)*, which, in speaking about the promises of obedience made at ordination in the context of priestly ministry being given only in communion with the pope and the college of bishops, amplifies the role of the diocesan bishop as one with whom a presbyter must have a special communion. We note in particular the expansion of the normal wording of the promise of obedience such that one's own diocesan bishop deserves "a kind of particular respect and obedience." Our official English translation further defines this particular relationship as a filial one. Here is the text:

"First of all, obedience is 'apostolic' in the sense that it recognizes, loves and serves the church in her hierarchical structure. Indeed, there can be no genuine priestly *(sacerdotale)* ministry except in communion with the supreme pontiff and the episcopal college *(in communione cum Summo Pontifice et cum collegio episcopali)*, especially with one's own diocesan bishop *(praesertim cum propriae dioecesis Episcopo)*, who deserves that 'filial respect and obedience' *(peculiaris quaedam reverentia atque obedientia)* promised during the rite of ordination. This 'submission' *(submissio)* to those invested with ecclesial authority is in no way a kind of humiliation. It flows from the responsible freedom of the priest *(presbyteri)*. . . .

"Authentic Christian obedience, when it is properly motivated and lived without servility, helps the priest *(presbyterum)* to exercise in accordance with the Gospel the authority entrusted to him for his work with the people of God: an authority free from authoritarianism *(sine auctoritatis scilicet abusu)* or demagoguery."[24]

It would seem that the use of "filial" in the English translation is both an attempt to give some definition to what kind of particular respect and obedience is owed the local bishop as well as a recalling of other texts of the Second Vatican Council such as *Lumen Gentium* 28, *Presbyterorum Ordinis* 15, and *Perfectae Caritatis* 14, studied in chapter 4, which define this relationship as filial. However, it is curious that John Paul did not use a more specific term in the Latin text. It opens the question as to what is intended here. In defining relationships, undefined terms can lead to confusion and even abuse.

Further, there is no attempt to understand priestly obedience as a relational or mutual reality. In fact, this text is exceedingly one-dimensional. It only speaks of the presbyters' special relationship to the bishop. There is no mention of the bishop's responsibility to his presbyters, to treat them as sons, etc. Then John Paul uses the term submission *(submissio)*, a term never used in the context of the promise of obedience in ordination rites. The use of subservience *(subjectio)* in medievel rites of ordination implied a feudal relationship, which has a dimension of mutuality. There seems here to be a clear intent to emphasize the bishop's control over his presbyters.

This one-dimensional understanding of obedience is further enhanced in the next paragraph, which speaks of authentic obedience as an authority free from authoritarianism or demagoguery. While presbyters are urged not to lord it over their people and abuse their power, there is no mention of bishops abusing their power. Unfortunately, abuse of power is a real issue to be confronted not only in every rectory but also in every chancery office and, most particularly, in the curial offices of the Vatican. Bishops and popes and the people who run their offices, as well as pastors and all who work in parishes, must take the temptation to power most seriously. Thus an opportu-

[24] "Pastores Dabo Vobis," 28, *Acta Apostolicae Sedis* 84 (1992) 701–2. English translation: *Origins* 21:45 (1992) pp. 717–59.

nity to give a proper understanding to the mutuality of obedience was missed.

John Paul continues in "I Will Give You Shepherds" 28 by saying that priestly obedience has a communitarian, ascetical, and pastoral dimension. These three dimensions seem to recall issues of religious life that are pertinent to all presbyters. In these paragraphs John Paul speaks of the unity of the presbyterate, which again includes both religious and diocesan presbyters. Since these issues are left in general terms, it would seem that this special promise of obedience for religious to the local bishop will be the source of much reflection in the future development of religious orders in the Church.

While much can be said about religious presbyters and their relationship to diocesan ministry, the further issue of how the promise of obedience of religious deacons to the local bishop is part of this ecclesiology is not so clear. There is the issue of religious deacons who share in the diaconate with the diocesan deacons, in particular with permanent deacons who minister in the same diocese. There is the reality that obedience for religious deacons, because of the structure of the order, is not the same as obedience for diocesan deacons.[25] This issue is further confused with the addition of a promise of celibacy for religious deacons. This promise of celibacy was added by the expressed wish of Pope John Paul II, against the exemption of canon 1037 of the 1983 Code of Canon Law,[26] and seems to be part of the desire to add to the importance of the vow of chastity by having it publicly renewed and proclaimed in this promise of celibacy. However, the issue here is that the vow of chastity and the promise of celibacy, while the same in their concrete lived-out realities, differ in their theological and eschatological signification in the spirituality of any given religious community. It seems that the Pope wished to place all ordained religious, that is, religious deacons and presbyters, more securely under the authority of the local diocesan bishop.[27] The implications concerning religious deacons making promises of obedience and celibacy to the local diocesan bishop, the relationship of these

[25] Lessi-Ariosto, "Commentarium," 107–8.

[26] Ibid., 107–8; Jounel, "La Nouvelle Édition Typique," 11. Kleinheyer, "Ordinationsfeiern," 112–3.

[27] This likewise seems to mean that canon 273 of the 1983 Code of Canon Law will need clarification. It simply states that clerics are bound by a special obligation to show reverence and obedience to the Supreme Pontiff and to their own

promises to the vows of obedience and chastity taken at profession, and how all this relates to any role religious deacons might take in the pastoral ministry of the local diocese are yet to be resolved. The issue is the relationship between religious life and holy orders. Religious orders have their own integrity above and beyond the boundaries and authority of a local diocese. Nevertheless, all ordained ministers in some sense are subject to the authority of the local bishop. The special promise of obedience for religious deacons along with the promise of celibacy to the local diocesan bishop makes a significant theological statement, one that will be the source of further reflection for members of religious orders who also share in holy orders.

Finally, there is the issue of personal prelatures. Personal prelatures are only mentioned once in the second typical edition, in the introduction proper to the rite of ordination of deacons,[28] where it states that the entrance to the clerical state and incardination into a diocese or personal prelature begins with diaconate. The creation of personal prelatures seems to find its precedent in the creation of the mendicant orders, especially the Dominicans.[29] Thus they are seen as a group who are exempt from local diocesan control and who are under papal authority. Both the historical precedent of the movement to diocesan control of the mendicant orders, which we studied in chapter 3, and the theological impetus of the Second Vatican Council to place all ordained ministry under the authority of the local diocesan bishop, and somewhat realized in the added promises of obedience in the second typical edition of the rites of ordination, seem to point to a possible further development in which the ordained members of personal prelatures will likewise be subject to the local diocesan bishop. In any case, this ritual development will play an essential role in the theological development of all ordained members of any religious order or personal prelature.

---

ordinary (*Clerici speciali obigatione tenentur Summo Pontifici et suo quisque Ordinario reverentiam et oboedientiam exhibendi*). Since this canon did not base obedience on the sacramental bond of orders, as do the council documents, this addition of a special promise of obedience for religious to the local bishop needs to be taken into account here. See the above quote from "Pastores Dabo Vobis" 28 and Schneider, "Obedience to the Bishop," 246–54.

[28] *De Ordinatione, Episcopi, Presbyterorum, et Diaconorum,* no. 176.

[29] Fox, "Personal Prelature of the Second Vatican Council," 67.

ECCLESIOLOGICAL REFLECTIONS

At first reading the small addition of a special promise of obedience for religious to the local diocesan bishop seems to be a blatant power move on the part of local bishops to exert more control over the religious who work in their diocese. However, it is now more likely that this ritual addition is a logical development flowing out of the ecclesiology of the council documents. In fact, these promises seem to be a significant theological statement that help to clarify the ongoing issues of the relationship between diocesan and religious presbyters and their relationship to the local diocesan bishop. In the proper understanding of *lex orandi, lex credendi,* this small liturgical addition will play a major role in the theological development and discussion of orders.

At this point it may be advantageous to both regress a little into history and project a little into the future. In the history of both the monastic orders and the mendicant experiment, the issue of ordained religious presbyters and their relationship to local bishops was neither a theological nor a sacramental one. Those monks who were ordained presbyters were ordained presbyters for the needs of their local monastery. The issues here only involved who had the power to ordain and who had the power to grant the faculties for ministry. Here we have the long and unique history of the power of exempt abbots and exempt monasteries. The mendicants were under papal authority and control. They received faculties to minister from the pope. Even projecting our contemporary sacramental issues of how these presbyters shared in the one priesthood of Christ with the bishops, there would not have been a major concern. Monks enjoyed the sense of the unity of the local monastic community and mendicants enjoyed the sense of the universal mandate from the pope. However, with the rise of so many religious orders from around the time of the Council of Trent until our time, the construct of priestly ministry has changed. If religious presbyters only need faculties to function as priests, the local bishop can oblige. If religious presbyters need to understand how their priesthood is a sharing in the one priesthood of Christ with the local bishop, this becomes confusing. It is further confused with the reality that with the shortage of priests more and more religious presbyters are doing normal parish ministry. Is not a religious presbyter, as pastor of a parish in a diocese, in terms of the sacramentality of his priesthood, more like a diocesan priest than a religious? That is the crux of the issue. Religious presbyters who serve the needs of a parish in a diocese should realize their priesthood in unity with the local bishop. Thus we have these developments in the rites of ordination.

Projecting into the future, it would seem that the future of religious life will depend on the radical living out of community life more than on priestly ordination. It would seem that the various religious orders need to return to their original charisms, live in community, concentrate on specialized ministry, and perhaps only ordain those numbers needed to serve their needs. Likewise, it would seem that their ministry would be much more localized, meeting particular needs in particular places. Perhaps stability needs a second look as an important community vow. In our highly mobile and inconstant world a group of men and women living out part of the radical message of Jesus in one part of the globe is an essential part of the evangelizing and re-evangelizing mission of the Church.

Finally, we must say a word about abuse of power and control issues. We can speak eloquently about the theological and spiritual qualities of an obedience lived out in service to God's people. However, the reality of human sinfulness makes any relationship with authority both fragile and tenuous. Those in authority must be vigilant to ensure that both the good of the Church and its people as well as the good of those who minister under them will be honored. Any decisions made without these considerations will be seen as abusive and harmful. Religious orders, in particular those religious ordained presbyters, have a prophetic and charismatic role to play in the mission of the Church. It is critical that bishops, who represent the hierarchical Church, allow much freedom for the Holy Spirit to work in the various orders and movements in the Church.

While there are still further unresolved issues, like the possibility of expressing the theological distinction between presbyter and deacon in the wording of the promise of obedience and the relationship between the promises of obedience and celibacy for religious deacons and their vows of profession, the enhancement of the reality of the local diocese as the local church under the authority of the local bishop is a welcome development. This development strengthens the power of the local bishop, but in terms of his call to the service of the people of his diocese. This is a small but important development in the theological and canonical understanding of the authority and dignity of each diocesan bishop and his relationship to the authority and power of the pope.

Finally, it seems advantageous that the various episcopal conferences and episcopal committees for the various language groups take special care to reflect on the ritual expression of these various promises of obedience and adapt both the wording and the gestures well. This seems to be a unique chance for the cultural adaptation of the Roman Rite, in the various vernacular translations, to further the theological development of the Church's understanding of holy orders and how obedience is ritualized for the good order of the Church.

Eastern Rites and Eastern Catholic Churches

A short inclusion of Eastern ordination rites, specifically since they concern Eastern Catholic churches, is necessary for catholicity. However, the first and most significant point is that there are no promises of obedience in any of the Eastern rites of ordination.[1] As in the West for the first millennium, the issues of obedience were part of the broader commitment to serve the needs of the Church, and thus it was not necessary to ritualize them in the rites of ordination.

The major area of interest is the relationship between bishops and their patriarch, and for the Eastern Catholic churches, the relationship of their patriarchs, and indeed all bishops, with the Bishop of Rome. Since the major developments in these areas are rather recent, we begin with the 1957 codification of law for Eastern Catholic churches in the motu proprio entitled *Cleri Sanctitati*, proceed to the Decree on the Eastern Catholic Churches *(Orientalium Ecclesiarum)* of the Second Vatican Council, and finally progress to the most recent 1990 Codes of Canons of the Eastern churches.

CLERI SANCTITATI

This motu proprio of Pius XII is a response to the unique traditions of Eastern Catholic churches after the publication of the 1917 Code of Canon Law. In chapter 3, subtitled "Obligations of Clerics," Canon 63 speaks of the obligation of obedience of clerics to their bishops or hierarchs. Hierarch is a particular Eastern term for one's clerical superior.

---

[1] An easy collection of Eastern ordination rites may be found in Lodi, *Enchiridion Euchologicum Fontium Liturgicorum*, 1348–70.

"All clerics, but chiefly priests *(presbyteri)*, are under the special obligation to show respect and obedience *(reverentiam et obedientiam exhibendi)* each to his own Hierarch. The Hierarchs, however, shall be mindful that they are fathers, not lords, and they shall therefore treat the clergy with fatherly affection."[2]

The first sentence is a repeat of Canon 127 of the 1917 Code of Canon Law, which clearly uses terms taken from the rite of ordination of presbyters in the West. The issue here is that presbyters in the Eastern rites do not make a promise of obedience. The second sentence, containing the description of the role of the bishop as one who is a father and not a lord, is an Eastern addition and seems to be part of the fuller understanding of the reciprocal nature of obedience, and thus is a significant text. This is especially true as these images will become part of the theology of obedience in some of the texts of the Second Vatican Council. Here these images seem to be part of the long tradition of relating obedience to monastic ideals, a tradition that continues to have significant meaning in the East.[3]

Obedience as part of the broader commitment to serve the needs of the Church under the guidance of the bishop is further clarified in Canon 64. This canon is an exact repeat of Canon 128 in the 1917 Code:

"As often and as long as the need of the Church requires it, in the judgment of their proper Hierarch, clerics are obliged, excepting a legitimate impediment, faithfully to carry out the duty with which they are charged by the Hierarch."[4]

Here, in the broader context of serving the needs of the Church, a mature response is expected, as implied in "excepting a legitimate impediment." Obedience is neither blind nor autocratic. Again, the reciprocal nature of obedience seems to be supported.

We turn now to chapter 6, which is entitled "Patriarchs." Canon 216 gives both the context and the understanding of the powers of patriarchs:

---

[2] "Cleri Sanctitati," *Acta Apostolicae Sedis* 49 (1957) 455. English translation: Pospishil, *Code of Oriental Canon Law*, 65.

[3] Pospishil, *Code of Oriental Canon Law*, 65.

[4] "Cleri Sanctitati," 455. Pospishil, *Code of Oriental Canon Law*, 66.

"1. Special respect is due to the patriarchs of the East, in accordance with the oldest tradition of the Church, since they preside each his own patriarchate or Rite as father and head with the most ample powers *(amplissima potestate)*, granted or recognized *(data seu agnita)* by the Roman Pontiff.

"2.1. The title of patriarch is given to a bishop to whom the canons assign jurisdiction *(cui canones tribuunt iurisdiction)* over all other bishops, including metropolitans, the clergy and the faithful of a territory or Rite, to be exercised under the authority of the Roman Pontiff, according to the norms of law *(ad normam iuris, sub auctoritate Romani Pontificis)*.

"2.2. Patriarchs possess authority over the faithful of the same Rite who reside outside the boundaries of their territory to the extent it is determined expressly in general or particular law."[5]

After stating the antiquity of the tradition of patriarchs, we are told that they have full power, which is either granted or recognized by the Roman pontiff. While this represents some of the ambiguity of the history of Eastern Catholic churches in union with Rome, it still maintains the ancient tradition of Eastern churches having their own apostolic authority, an authority to be recognized by the Roman pontiff. This tradition seems to be affirmed in the statement that a patriarch is a bishop to whom the canons assign jurisdiction over all other bishops in his territory or rite. However, this same statement seems to limit this jurisdiction by placing it under the authority of the Roman pontiff. Finally, patriarchs have authority over the faithful of their rite who live outside their territory, according to the various laws.

Canons 221 to 244 deal with the election of the patriarch, an ancient Eastern tradition, similar in essence to the election of the Bishop of Rome by the conclave of cardinals. Of interest is Canon 236, which deals with the relationship between the newly elected patriarch and the Roman pontiff. It includes informing the Roman pontiff of the election, a profession of faith, an oath of fidelity, and a request for ecclesiastical communion and for the pallium.

"1. The new patriarch must send a report to the Roman Pontiff concerning the election, together with the documents, signed by himself,

---

[5] "Cleri Sanctitati," 497. Pospishil, *Code of Oriental Canon Law,* 114.

the profession of faith *(professione fidei)* made by him according to approved forms in the presence of the synod, and the oath of fidelity *(deque iureiurando fidelitatis)*, and at the same time request ecclesiastical communion and the pallium, which is an insignia of the fullness of the pontifical office *(plenitudinis officii pontificalis insigne)."*[6]

The profession of faith seems to mean the profession of the creed. The oath of fidelity would include an act of obedience to the Roman pontiff. The request for ecclesiastical communion is an acknowledgment of the unitive function of the Bishop of Rome as a sign of the catholicity of the whole Church. The pallium is a sign of the fullness of the pontifical office, which the patriarch possesses. What is important here is that the process for the election is dependent on the local church and not the Roman pontiff, and it is the local church that has the responsibility of seeking and maintaining union with the whole Church.

In part 2, chapter 1, concerning the election of bishops, Canon 392 states that bishops are successors of the apostles and are under the authority of the Roman pontiff, who appoints them freely or confirms those legitimately elected. This is a repeat of Canon 329 of the 1917 Code except for the final statement, here in italics, which was added to cover the election of bishops by the local churches in the Eastern tradition:

"2. They are freely appointed by the Roman Pontiff, *or if lawfully elected, confirmed by him (aut legitime electos confirmat)."*[7]

It will be important to keep these two traditions, a bishop freely appointed by Rome and one legitimately elected by the local church, in mind as we study the development of the naming of bishops in the Eastern Catholic churches. Here these two traditions seem to be equal in stature. One significant note is that in the 1983 Latin Code of Canon Law, this canon, with its mention of these two traditions, will be included in Canon 377, an acknowledgment of the older tradition in the West of bishops being elected by the local church.

In Canon 395 these two traditions are overshadowed by the necessity that every bishop, even those elected, receive a canonical provi-

[6] "Cleri Sanctitati," 503. Pospishil, *Code of Oriental Canon Law,* 121.
[7] "Cleri Sanctitati," 548. Pospishil, *Code of Oriental Canon Law,* 175.

sion that only the Roman pontiff can grant. This serves the same purpose as the papal mandate necessary for the ordination of a bishop in
the Roman Rite. Before they can receive this canonical provision, they
must also take an oath of fidelity to the Apostolic See. This seems to
follow the Tridentine order of an oath of fidelity sent to Rome some-
time before the ordination of a bishop. Here an eparchy is an Eastern
term for a territory over which a bishop can have authority.

"1. Every candidate for the episcopate, even those elected or desig-
nated in virtue of a grant by the Roman Pontiff in concordats or otherwise, needs the canonical provision by which he becomes the bishop
of the vacant eparchy, and which is granted solely by the Roman
Pontiff. . . .

"2. The candidate must take, before the canonical provision, besides
the profession of faith (fidei professionem), an oath of fidelity (iusiurandum fidelitatis) to the Apostolic See according to the formula approved
by the Apostolic See."[8]

We need to keep both the emphasis and the wording in mind as we
study the development of the understanding of Eastern bishops to the
Bishop of Rome. However, at this time there seems to be clear evidence of the Romanization of the election process of Eastern Catholic
bishops and patriarchs, an imbalance the Second Vatican Council attempted to redress.

ORIENTALIUM ECCLESIARUM

The Second Vatican Council decree on the Eastern Catholic
churches reaffirms the antiquity, richness, equality, and dignity of the
many Eastern Catholic churches. In speaking of their relationship to
the Roman pontiff, an effort is made to maintain a balance between
the authority of the Bishop of Rome and the authority of each Eastern
Catholic church. *Orientalium Ecclesiarum* 3 nuances the sense of the
authority of the Roman pontiff over Eastern Catholic churches with
the use of different terms such as the "pastoral guidance" of the
Roman pontiff and "under the direction" of the Roman Pontiff.[9] *Orientalium Ecclesiarum* 5 states that Eastern Catholic churches have the

---

[8] "Cleri Sanctitati," 549. Pospishil, *Code of Oriental Canon Law,* 176.
[9] Tanner, *Decrees of the Ecumenical Councils,* 2:901.

right to govern themselves in accordance with their own particular disciplines.

Now we turn to the treatment of patriarchs, which in the judgment of some is poor because of what it chooses not to cover.[10] Nevertheless, *Orientalium Ecclesiarum* 7 develops the contents of the text of Canon 216 of *Cleri Sanctitati* in a manner consistent with the basic teaching of the decree.

"The patriarchal function has been flourishing in the church from the earliest times, already recognized by the first ecumenical synods.

"By the term 'eastern patriarch' is meant a bishop who possesses jurisdiction *(cui competit iurisdictio)* over all the bishops (including metropolitans), clergy and faithful of his own territory or rite in accordance with the norm of law and without prejudice to the primacy of the Roman Pontiff *(salvo primatu Romani Pontificis.)*"[11]

First of all, the notion of the power of the patriarch as either given or recognized by the Roman pontiff, as found in *Cleri Sanctitati,* is replaced here with the notion of the recognition of the institution of patriarchs by the earliest councils. Second, the concept of patriarchs being assigned jurisdiction by their own canons in *Cleri Sanctitati* is here replaced with a simple statement of the patriarch as one who possesses jurisdiction. This leaves the whole historical question of jurisdiction very much open.[12] Finally, the sense of the authority of the Roman pontiff is nuanced, such that the phrase "under the authority of the Roman Pontiff" is modified here as "without prejudice to the primacy of the Roman Pontiff."

Orientalium Ecclesiarum 9 begins by again quoting Canon 216 of *Cleri Sanctitati,* but omits, as in article 7, the notion of the power of the patriarch as either given or recognized by the Roman pontiff. It calls for the ancient rights and privileges of the Eastern Catholic churches to be restored in accordance with their traditions. Then follows this significant statement:

"The patriarchs with their synods make up a higher tribunal for all matters concerning the patriarchate, including the right of setting up

[10] J. Hoeck in Vorgrimler, *Commentary on the Documents of Vatican II,* 1:319.

[11] Tanner, *Decrees of the Ecumenical Councils,* 902.

[12] Hoeck, in Vorgrimler, *Commentary on the Documents of Vatican II,* 1:320.

new eparchies and of appointing new bishops of their own rite within the confines of their own patriarchal territory, without prejudice to the inalienable right of the Roman pontiff of intervening in individual cases (*salvo inalienabili Romani Pontificis iure in singulis casibus interveniendi*)."[13]

In particular, patriarchs with their synods are the highest authority for all matters concerning the patriarchate. In the Eastern patriarchal structure, the patriarch cannot act outside the will of his local synod. This authority includes the right to set up new eparchies and to appoint new bishops for their rite, again without prejudice to the inalienable right of the Roman pontiff to intervene in individual cases.

In would seem that in the texts of *Orientalium Ecclesiarum* there was a concerted effort to maintain the valid traditions of the Eastern Catholic churches and to nuance their relationship with the valid authority of the Roman pontiff. However, the final text seems to be a compromise,[14] and the ramifications of Eastern Catholic churches using fully their apostolic authority have yet to be experienced. This is particularly true in the present structure for the selection of bishops for Eastern Catholic churches. As in the West, a serious look at a return to a true metropolitan structure for the selection, ordination, and overseeing of suffragan bishops seems to be worthy of our counciliar commitment to return to our apostolic roots. It would likewise seem that for the East, as for the West, the further study of the metropolitan structure is essential for a deeper theological understanding of the relationship between all bishops, metropolitans, and patriarchs with the Bishop of Rome.

CODE OF CANONS OF THE EASTERN CHURCHES

This codification, completed in 1990, should show the fruit of a generation of reflection on the teachings of the Second Vatican Council that the ancient rights and privileges of the Eastern Catholic churches be restored. With this hope in mind, we turn to the canons on patriarchal churches. In Canon 55 we find a consolidation of Canon 216 in *Cleri Sanctitati* and its abridgement in *Orientalium Ecclesiarum* 7, in which patriarchal institutions are seen as ancient and worthy of honor. The issue of patriarchal power, not covered in *Orientalium Ecclesiarum*, is given a nuanced treatment in Canon 56.

[13] Tanner, *Decrees of the Ecumenical Councils*, 903.
[14] Hoeck, in Vorgrimler, *Commentary on the Documents of Vatican II*, 1:321.

"A patriarch is a bishop who enjoys power over all bishops including metropolitans and other Christian faithful of the Church over which he presides according to the norm of law approved by the supreme authority of the Church *(ad normam iuris a suprema Ecclesiae auctoritate approbati)*."[15]

What is significant here is the statement that patriarchs have power "according to the norm of law approved by the supreme authority of the Church." This is an important change from Canon 216 of *Cleri Sanctitati*, where patriarchs exercised their powers "under the authority of the Roman Pontiff." This seemingly would allow for the tradition of the autonomy of Eastern synodal authority to be respected, especially in the election of patriarchs and bishops.

Concerning the election of patriarchs and the notification of the Roman pontiff, Canon 76 is basically a repeat of Canon 236 of *Cleri Sanctitati*, except that the oath of fidelity is replaced with a promise to exercise his office with fidelity in the presence of the synod according to the approved formulas:

"1. By means of a synodal letter, the synod of bishops of the patriarchal Church notifies the Roman Pontiff as soon as possible about the canonical conduct of the election and enthronement and that the new patriarch made a profession of faith *(professione fidei)* and the promise to exercise his office with fidelity *(promissione fideliter officium suum implendi)* in the presence of the synod according to the approved formulas."[16]

Again, this seems to allow a return to a more autonomous understanding of authority for the synodal process.

Nevertheless, in Canon 92 we find a clear description of the relationship between patriarch and the Roman pontiff, one that includes the obedience implied in an oath of fidelity.

"1. The patriarch is to manifest hierarchical communion with the Roman Pontiff, successor of St. Peter, through the loyalty, veneration and obedience *(per fidelitatem, venerationem et oboedientiam)* which are due to the supreme pastor of the entire Church."[17]

[15] *Code of Canons of the Eastern Churches*, 24.
[16] Ibid., 31–2.
[17] Ibid., 40.

However, here fidelity, veneration, and obedience are seen in the context of the hierarchical communion required of bishops with the Bishop of Rome, successor of Peter. This seems to be a more theological understanding of this important relationship, one that aids the ongoing discussion of this issue, since it is unique to this code.

Turning to the election of bishops,[18] Canon 181 states that the nomination and election of bishops inside the territorial boundaries of the patriarchal church is the responsibility of the local synod. Then it declares that other bishops are to be appointed by the Roman pontiff. This canon is significant for two reasons. First, it returns this process to the local synod. This is meant to be the norm for the election of local bishops. Second, it inverts the order of Canon 392 of *Cleri Sanctitati*. Now the election of bishops by the local synod is the primary means of election, and the appointment of bishops by the Roman pontiff is a secondary means.[19]

While all bishops elected by local synods are to be approved or confirmed by the Roman pontiff, nevertheless, how this important aspect is understood is somewhat understated and nuanced in the various canons. It seems that in the normal course of events the names of three candidates, proposed by the synod, are to be sent to the Roman pontiff for approval before the election process takes place. Once a candidate is elected, confirmation by the Roman pontiff is assumed. This is the context of Canons 168 and 182.[20] Canon 182.3 states that candidates for bishop are to obtain the assent of the Roman pontiff, a term that seems to allow more responsibility on the part of the synod. In more particular circumstances, the Roman pontiff plays a more active role. Canon 149, which deals with the election of bishops outside the territorial boundaries of the patriarchal Church, has the synod sending three candidates to the Roman pontiff, who will appoint one. Thus, in general, the return to the synodal process of election of bishops is supported.

Finally, Canon 187 states that canonical provision is necessary for anyone to be elected a bishop in the Eastern Catholic churches. It is also here that specific reference is made concerning a promise of obedience to the Roman pontiff:

[18] See Khoury, "The Election of Bishops in the Eastern Churches," 20–27.

[19] R. Metz, "La désignation des évêques dans le droit actuel: étude comparative entre le Code latin de 1983 et le Code oriental de 1990," 327.

[20] Pospishil, *Eastern Catholic Church Law*, 163–4.

"2. Prior to episcopal ordination the candidate is to make a profession faith and a promise of obedience *(professionem fidei necnon promissionem oboedientiae)* to the Roman Pontiff and, in patriarchal Churches, also a promise of obedience *(promissionem oboedientiae)* to the patriarch in those matters in which he is subject *(subiectus)* to the patriarch according to the norm of law."[21]

We seem to have a definite development of the text of Canon 395 of *Cleri Sanctitati,* which uses the terminology of making an oath of fidelity to the Apostolic See. Now both a profession of faith and a promise of obedience are to be sent to the Roman pontiff. This reflects the decision of the part of the authors of the 1990 Code to favor the use of such terms as "promise of obedience" and "Roman Pontiff."[22] This is a change from Canon 380 in the 1983 Latin Code of Canon Law, which, in the similar context of a bishop taking canonical possession of his office, states that the bishop is to make a profession of faith and take "an oath of fidelity to the Apostolic See." Thus we have a conscious effort to return to the older vocabulary of making promises and the maintaining of the older Western practice of bishops sending a promise of obedience to the pope, an act separate from the ordination rite.

Finally, the promise of obedience made to the Roman pontiff is placed in the context of the promise of obedience made to the patriarch, according to the norm of law. This is the first time a promise of obedience to the patriarch by suffragan bishops is specifically mentioned, and without further explanation. We are not told how this promise is made. While such obedience has always been understood as necessary for good ministry in the Church, it would seem that how obedience is ritualized here is worthy of much more thought. However, the general metropolitan structure is supported and maintained.

In the case of either promise of obedience, there is no thought of adding a ritual promise of obedience to the rite of ordination. This confirms the basic fact that ritual promises of obedience are late Western additions to rites of ordination, and perhaps their role in ordination rites needs to be given serious reconsideration.

[21] *Code of Canons of the Eastern Churches,* 90.
[22] Metz, "La désignation des évêques dans le droit actuel," 332.

The desire of the teachings of the Second Vatican Council for the restoration of the rights and privileges of the Eastern Catholic churches in accordance with their traditions, actions that will strengthen the patriarchal structures of these churches, is one of paramount importance not only for the Eastern Catholic churches but for the great hope of the reunion of all the Orthodox churches with the See of Peter. One small part of this patriarchal autonomy concerns the election of bishops and their relationship with the Roman pontiff. This issue of the metropolitan structure of churches is ancient as well in the West, and thus they are related issues. It would seem that development in one part of the Church will benefit the whole. Paraphrasing the words of Pope John Paul II, the Church needs to breath with both its lungs.

Conclusions

In these last pages we hope to summarize our conclusions and articulate the questions yet to be resolved. First of all, we recall the intrinsic nature of Christian obedience. Obedience to the will of the Father is the basis of all Christian life. Likewise, obedience is a relational and dynamic term, one that demands that we both listen and respond to the Word of God Incarnate who is Jesus Christ.

Obedience has always been an intrinsic part of the nature of the ministerial structure of the Church. Apostles were sent, bishops were chosen, presbyters were called, and deacons were needed, all because obedience to the will of God, ascertained in prayer, determined these ministers were essential for the work of the Church.

THE HISTORICAL CONTEXT OF THE PROMISE OF OBEDIENCE: THE STRUCTURAL FREEDOM OF THE CHURCH

In general, for the first millennia of the Church there was no need to ritualize this essential element as part of the rituals of ordained ministry in the Church. Likewise, in the early promises that made up monastic profession, obedience to the abbot, and indeed to one another, was implied as an essential part of monastic life, and thus there was no need to explicitly mention obedience to the abbot in those rituals.

The beginnings of the ritualization of obedience seem to be found in the development of the pallium at Rome. The pallium was a sign of the authority of the pope. As the various local churches struggled with local rulers for the freedom to minister their churches, one solution was the sending of the pallium by the pope to the local archbishop as a sign that this archbishop was under the authority of the pope and therefore free from interference by the local lord. Thus the local archbishop and the local church were structurally free to be Church.

Beginning with Boniface, the apostle to the Franks, we find a promise of obedience to the pope connected to the bestowal of the pallium, and with this promise we have the beginning of the development of the long tradition of bishops making a promise of obedience to the pope. Again, the purpose of this promise of obedience was the structural freedom of the Church.

In the churches of the kingdom of the Franks many of the local archbishops began to seek promises of obedience from their suffragan bishops, again in order to free those bishops and their dioceses from interference by the local lords. Likewise, many bishops began to ask for a promise of obedience from their priests, following the example of vassalage to a feudal lord, as part of the solution to the issue of proprietary churches. This allowed the local parishes to be under the authority of the local bishop and thus free from the politics of the ruling lord.

THE PROMISE OF OBEDIENCE IN THE PONTIFICALS: THE MOVEMENT TOWARD A JURIDICAL NOTION OF OBEDIENCE

It was in Germany that we find a promise of obedience in the rites of ordination for the first time in the tenth-century pontifical that is known as the Romano-Germanic. Presbyters were asked to make a promise of obedience to their bishop, and bishops were asked to make a promise of obedience to the pope. The promise of obedience found its logical place as part of the examination that preceded the actual ordination.

In Rome there would be no promises of obedience in the actual rites of ordination of presbyters until the adoption of the Pontifical of William Durandus following the return of the popes from Avignon in the fourteenth century. The rites of ordination in this pontifical seem to be a compilation of the best of both traditions, Roman and German. Included for the first time as part of the gesture of the promise of obedience in the ordination rite of presbyters was the joining of the hands, a ritual from the old feudal structure of vassalage. The *immixtio manuum* seems to have first become part of the promises of obedience in mendicant rites of profession and thus influenced this development in rites of ordination.

There were several developments in the Pontifical of William Durandus that point to significant changes in both ecclesiology and theology. First of all, the examination was either shortened or moved, resulting in the moving of the promise of obedience for both presbyters and bishops. For presbyters it was now part of a series of rituals done after Communion. For bishops it was part of the examination and promises made prior to the rite of ordination. In either case, the connection of the ritual promise of obedience to the rites of ordination was diminished.

For presbyters the movement of the promise of obedience to the series of rituals after Communion seems to indicate the movement to a more juridical understanding of obedience, one that emphasized the giving of the faculties to celebrate the Eucharist and to hear confessions. This development would simply be made part of both the teachings and rituals of the Council of Trent.

THE DIMINISHMENT OF THE METROPOLITAN STRUCTURE: THE MOVEMENT TOWARD PAPAL CENTRALIZATION

In the ordination rites of bishops, the most significant development was the loss of the metropolitan structure. While the Pontifical of William Durandus still makes mention of the local metropolitan as one to whom suffragan bishops owe obedience as well as to the pope, by the time we arrive at the rites of Trent this element is lacking in the ritual expression of obedience. This was part of the development of papal authority that began with the reforms of Gregory VII and the general acceptance of the Decretals of Gratian. Bishops could appeal directly to the pope concerning their relationships with any other bishop or archbishop. As the papacy became more centralized, it likewise played a greater role in the selection of bishops. With the reforms of Trent this centralized structure becomes complete. It would seem advantageous for our time to enhance the role of the metropolitan, the archbishop of a province, in the naming of bishops in the province as well as in the ritual expressions of the rite of episcopal ordination. This would allow for the local church and its leaders to take greater leadership in naming new shepherds. This greater leadership should allow for greater responsibility for those who are called to be true teachers and pontiffs of their dioceses. While a certain amount of centralization has structural advantages, the present system of papal appointment of bishops tends to foster too much dependency on the pope for decision making in all areas, a loss of some of the rich diversity of gifted leadership in the Church. We need a new look at the concept of the Petrine ministry of the pope as one who confirms his brothers in the ministry, a ministry as varied as the people who make up the Church.

THE HISTORICAL DEVELOPMENT
OF THE *PROMITTIS–PROMITTO* FORM

One final element worthy of mention is the development of the concept of a personal promise of obedience and its various will you–I will *(vis–volo)* and do you promise–I promise *(promittis–promitto)* forms used in the various rites of ordination. While the Romano-Germanic Pontifical used the *vis–volo* form, it seems that, influenced by the long tradition of promises in monastic rites of profession, which used the more personal *promitto*, a tradition then further developed by the mendicant orders. With the Pontifical of William Durandus we have a return in the ordination rite of presbyters to the use of *promittis–promitto*, the form presently in use in our rites of ordination. It would seem that further study on the form and wording such a promise could take for the adaptation of the 1990 second typical edition by the various episcopal conferences and language groups is of primary importance. Likewise, such a promise could be a telling moment in the rite, the moment when the one to be ordained publicly commits himself to obediently serve the people of his diocese and to be obedient to the vision of ministry of his bishop. Too often an ordination can seem, with all the temptation to grandness in ceremony, more like a promotion to power than a call to service. Ritually, this moment of obedience, in the form of a more personal promise, could counter such temptations with both wording and gestures that radically call both the candidates being ordained and indeed the entire assembly to follow the Lord. The present promise of obedience and respect to the bishop and his successors does not speak to the greater issues of obedient service in the Church today, an obedience that goes well beyond bishop and presbyter.

THE TEACHINGS OF THE SECOND VATICAN COUNCIL
ON HOLY ORDERS

The Second Vatican Council in its teachings on orders is a rich source of theological and ecclesiological reflection for ministry in the

Church. First of all, the council returned to the understanding of the bishop as possessing the fullness of orders. Furthermore, it taught that presbyters share in the priesthood of their bishops and are cooperators with them in the essential work of the building up of the Church. This inversion of the medieval understanding of orders has had a significant influence on both our theology of priesthood and how we celebrate rites of ordination. Theologically, the question of how a presbyter shares in the priesthood of his bishop, specifically in light of how we understand the traditional distinction of power and jurisdiction, is the most significant of unresolved issues. However, the greatest theological treasure here is the unity of priestly service. The more that people can see bishops and presbyters working in unity for the building up of the Church, the more the saving mission of Christ Jesus will be realized. Too often there is the temptation for both bishops and presbyters to be seen, and often they see themselves as lone rangers working as individuals with a solitary mission. Too many parishes have sacramental policies that differ from their neighboring parishes. Too many presbyters are perceived as not able to work well with other presbyters, a perception that damages the Church's unity. While there are issues to be resolved with this understanding of the sacramentality of orders, it seems that the advantages far outweigh the disadvantages.

THE RELATIONSHIP BETWEEN DIOCESAN AND RELIGIOUS PRESBYTERS AND THE DIOCESAN BISHOP

The one issue that has undergone the most significant development since the Second Vatican Council is the relationship between diocesan and religious presbyters and their relationship to the local diocesan bishop. The teachings of the council, with its emphasis on all presbyters, diocesan and religious, sharing with the bishops and in particular with their local diocesan bishop in the one priesthood of Christ, its emphasis on the diocese as the local church, and its emphasis on the local diocesan bishop as responsible for pastoral and liturgical ministry in his diocese, has given rise to a significant change in both the ecclesial reality and ritual expression of the promise of obedience taken at ordination for religious presbyters. While there are theological and historical reasons and precedents for these recent developments, the ramifications of these developments will not be immediately comprehended. It would seem that religious presbyters the fruits of this development in the renewal of the charisms respective orders. This renewal will allow them to both respond to the needs of the Church and to live obediently as sons in the hierarchical Church. Likewise, respect for the charisms of the various religious orders will allow bishops to respect the invaluable role that religious play in the mission of the Church. Nevertheless, there is the issue of control and the temptation to power. The greatest danger in the next years will be the possibility that some religious orders and their genuine charisms will be stifled or even crushed by some well-intentioned and some not so well-intentioned bishops. The central and indeed only hope is that whatever is of the Holy Spirit will remain.

THE DEVELOPMENT OF THE INTENT OF THE PROMISE OF OBEDIENCE IN ORDINATION RITES

Turning in particular to the promises of obedience in rites of ordination, we can articulate some observations concerning their intended role and purpose. As we summarized above, the initial purpose of promises of obedience was the placing of the various local dioceses and parishes under ecclesial authority to free the Church from the political interference of the local kings and lords. When this historical reality changed, the role of the promise of obedience took on a diminished ritual role, finding itself outside the actual rites of ordination. However, it took on a more theologically significant role, one that was understood as a major element in the ongoing development of the distinction between the power of ordination and the jurisdiction to function as bishop or presbyter.

At the time of the Second Vatican Council the promise of obedience as part of the rites of ordination was accepted as a matter of fact. The major issue for the promise of obedience in the reforms of ordination rites was where to place it in the rites themselves. As a result, a theological and ritual symmetry was decided upon in which all three orders would include promises of obedience as part of the examination immediately preceding the rite of ordination.

However, flowing out of the rich theological teachings of the council on orders, the promise of obedience, especially that of a presbyter to his bishop, was seen more as a sacramental statement of their sharing in the one priesthood of Christ than the canonical statement of a juridical reality. While the canonical issues of jurisdiction and faculties remain, and while both diocesan and religious presbyters depend on the bishops for the power to exercise their ministry, the emphasis is now more centered on the ecclesial reality of a local church, under its bishop, in communion with the universal Church, in which all the presbyters strive to build up the body of Christ. Thus, it seems that we have returned to a more basic understanding of ecclesial obedience, one that is at the core of all Christian life and upon which all Christian ministry depends. This seems to be a significant development that should serve the Church and its ministers well.

OBEDIENCE AND MATURITY

The council also taught that obedience must be based on a mature commitment and help lead to a fuller maturity as sons and daughters of God. All who are involved in ministry in the Church must be respected as human persons imbued with the dignity worthy of both their baptism and their call. Thus, a return call to a reciprocal notion of obedience that reflects such a notion both in reality and in ritual is essential to the reform of the promise of obedience in rites of ordination. The old form of the joining of the hands carried such a ritual significance of reciprocity. Whatever new forms the adaptations of the revision of the second typical edition take, some sense of this reciprocity is essential.

Likewise, this reciprocity needs to be a reality that is lived out in ministry. This is an essential element of priestly formation. While bishops need to be solicitous for the good of their presbyters, presbyters have a like responsibility. If candidates for priesthood, or presbyters who were formed elsewhere and move into a diocese, are not able to accept the demands of obedience to serve the needs of the people in the context of the plan and vision of the local bishop, there is a serious problem. Maturity demands an honest look at one's gifts for ministry and the ability to treasure the gifts others bring to ministry. Obedience demands that all work together for the good of the Church in order to meet the needs of its people. Together these two elements give a healthy balance to the human issues of ministry in the context of the structure of the Church.

THE RELATIONSHIP BETWEEN BISHOPS AND THE POPE

Another major unresolved issue is the further development and understanding of the relationship between bishops, as the successors of the apostles, and the pope, as the successor of Peter. The documents of both Vatican councils and the ritual texts of episcopal ordination struggle to keep this relationship both balanced and theologically correct. The issue is not papal authority and how bishops relate to the primacy of the pope but how the pope relates to the authority of each bishop. Bishops are legates of Christ, not of the pope. The pope is to assert, support, and defend the authority of each bishop. Bishops are true teachers of the faith, pontiffs, and pastors. The ritual development for the promise of obedience of religious presbyters to the local diocesan bishop in the second typical edition seems to make a significant theological statement, not only about the future of religious life but also about the authority of the local bishop, one that strengthens that authority.

It would seem that in the future we could see the further strengthening of the authority of the local bishop in his role as pontiff and pastor of his diocese. It would likewise seem that a return to the traditional Western metropolitan structure of church governance could perhaps serve the needs of local diocesan churches better than the present highly centralized structure. The essential role in the selection, ordination, and overseeing of suffragan bishops by the local metropolitan, an ancient and strong element in our tradition, is an indispensable part of the election process of bishops, who seemingly would be more knowledgeable of the needs and more committed to the people of the diocese for which they are ordained.

THE ROLE OF THE EXAMINATION

The hope that candidates be well chosen for orders is part of the rationale for the development of the new examination for bishops in the 1968 typical edition. In fact, the examinations of all three rites of ordination have been expanded with the hope that both the worthiness of the candidate may be ascertained and the needs of the local church may be expressed. The introduction of the 1990 second typical edition allows for a further adaptation of the examination to incorporate this desire. While these public questions lend solemnity to the ritual, and certainly they lend solemnity to the promise of obedience, the need for the role of the local church to be expressed in the election of this man to the diaconate, the presbyterate, and especially to the episcopacy for the one who will be their next bishop is another significant issue, for those responsible for the vernacular translations of the rites of ordination, to consider as part of the normal cultural adaptation of rites. In many ways the role of the assembly in these examinations speaks of the importance of the local church to take responsibility for the calling and forming of its ministers. True ministers do not come, for long, from somewhere else!

THE RELATIONSHIP BETWEEN THE PROFESSION OF FAITH AND THE EXAMINATION

Another long tradition related to orders and the promise of obedience is the making of a personal profession of faith, or as it is called later, the taking of an oath of fidelity. In fact, in the rites of ordination, the examination is often the ritual expression of the content of the profession of faith. In general, a profession of faith is concerned that the candidate both believe and teach orthodox doctrine. It is likewise concerned that he make this commitment freely and be under no duress. Finally, often there is a personal expression of obedience to the pope or bishop to whom the profession is made.

This profession of faith contained the commitment to celibacy for all those petitioning for major orders until the 1972 motu proprio *Ad pascendum* moved it, making the commitment to celibacy a special rite to be publicly done prior to the ordination rite for deacons. For bishops, this profession of faith, prior to the 1968 reform, contained the promise of obedience to the pope, a promise which then became a public part of the examination. Thus, there is need for further study of the role of this profession of faith and its relationship to the examination in ordination rites.

A final issue concerning the ritual use of the profession of faith is that it is indeed the faith of the entire Church that the one to be ordained professes. It must reflect the positive faith of the Church in both what God has done and in what God will yet do. Any desire to use the profession of faith as a sort of doctrinal litmus test is not helpful. The belief we profess is too important for such a role.

OBEDIENCE AS RELATIONAL, DYNAMIC, AND RECIPROCAL

The major issue here is not the profession of a promise of obedience. The major issue is the need for this profession to be freely made and for it to flow out of the candidate's ability to make a mature faith commitment. In others words, the need is not so much for the Church to ask obedience of its ministers, a reality essential for church governance, but for those who are called to orders to freely commit themselves to service in the Church. This is the essential aspect of an obedience that is relational, dynamic, and reciprocal. The Church seems to be fairly clear on its expectations of those in ordained ministry. What is not so clear are the expectations of spiritual maturity demanded of those making such promises.

Partly this involves the issues of the spiritual formation of candidates for orders. It would seem that an understanding of the human maturity demanded by the lifelong commitments of obedience and celibacy is essential; likewise, a basic level of spiritual maturity seems absolutely necessary prior to any public celebration of these promises.

This involves a renewed sense of the unitive charism of leadership in the Church. Bishops and popes are called, by the very function of their offices, to be a sign of unity for all those under their authority and to be a source of confirmation for all those who work with them in the Church.

Again, a promise of obedience is relational, dynamic, and reciprocal. It demands an active role on the part of both the one making the promise and the one to whom the promise is made. It shapes the lives of both parties. The one making the promise should arrive at a more mature and humble understanding of what it means to follow Christ. The one to whom the promise is made should arrive at a more mature and humble understanding of what it means to lead and build up the body of Christ. Likewise, the one to whom the promise is made should arrive at a better understanding of how he is to confirm his brothers in ministry. Only then, it seems, can promises of obedience be professed and renewed in the spirit of faith, hope, and love expected by the call of Christ.

Here, again we need to remind all ministers of the temptation to power and the unfortunate reality of the abuse of power in all levels of church ministry. Presbyters must minister to their people in such a way that enables them to grow into the people God created them to be. Presbyters likewise must serve the Church and their bishops in such a way that enables the Church to prosper and the needs of its people to be met. However, bishops and popes and all who serve in their offices must be ever vigilant against the temptation to the abuse of power. All decision making must be founded on trust and good consultation with those knowledgeable of the issues. When there is conflict, sometimes a reality necessary for growth, only leaders respected for their gospel values and prayer life will be able to transcend the human limitations of the people involved and urge those for whom they are responsible to accept difficult decisions. Any decision not made in such a context is abusive.

THE PROMISE OF OBEDIENCE FOR DEACONS AND PRESBYTERS

One final issue to recall is the relationship between presbyters and deacons, specifically the theological distinction between these two orders, and how this relates to the ecclesial reality of their promise of obedience. At present the ritual expression of their promises of obedience is exactly the same. It would seem that some development of the promise of obedience for presbyters that would reflect more fully the priesthood and the ecclesial reality of the order of presbyters sharing in the priesthood of their bishop would be helpful. There does not seem to be an overriding reason for the repetition of the same promise of obedience when a deacon is ordained to the presbyterate.

With the presence, here in the United States, of so many permanent deacons, many of whom are married men, it would seem that further reflection on how these men can live out and give example of obedient service in the Church would be a great witness to married couples who struggle to understand obedience to Christ and each other in marriage. Again, obedience must be freeing if it is to be Christian. Permanent deacons who are married need to recall that their primary sacrament is that of marriage. They serve the Church as married men with the grace of both sacraments. It would also seem that their promise of obedience needs to reflect this unique reality of marriage and orders.

PROPOSALS FOR ADAPTATION

Now we can summarize some of the ritual issues that can be addressed in the translation and adaptation of the second typical edition into the various vernacular editions. This is part of the important work of the inculturation of the Roman Rite in the many cultures and languages of the world.

First of all, perhaps the *promitto* for the promise of obedience for deacons and presbyters and the *volo* for bishops could be developed into a longer, more personal form, one that would be orally professed by the candidate and would reflect more theologically the significance of this commitment.

Second, the promise of obedience can be significantly different for deacons and presbyters, allowing for a promise that would reflect the theological distinctions between these two orders. Likewise, some mention of the ecclesial reality of the local diocese would be helpful.

Third, the promise of obedience could be professed in such a way that the reciprocity between the one making the promise and the one to whom the promise is made could be enhanced. It would seem that the commitment of the bishop to his presbyters and deacons and likewise of the pope to the bishops are elements presently lacking and perhaps needed for our time.

Finally, an expansion of the entire examination that could enhance the role of the community in the election of these candidates for all three orders would be a happy development. This expansion might allow for a better expression of the reciprocity between the candidate and the local church, such that the general ministerial needs of the local church could be more amply mentioned and the general desire of the candidates to meet those needs could be proclaimed.

MAJOR UNRESOLVED ISSUES

Finally, we conclude by stating those issues that remain and are yet to be resolved. Theologically, the issue of our understanding of the traditional distinction between order and jurisdiction is primary. Our understanding of how presbyters share in the priesthood of their bishop hinges on this issue. More significantly, how religious presbyters share in the priesthood of the local diocesan bishop hinges on this issue. While we have radically inverted our understanding of the relationship between bishop and presbyter since the events of the Second Vatican Council, the ramifications of this change are still to be comprehended. Ritually, the promise of obedience for religious presbyters and deacons to the local diocesan bishop is one significant theological statement in the ongoing development of this issue.

The second significant issue is that of the relationship between bishop and pope. It would seem that the loss of the major role played by metropolitans in the governance of the Church is lamentable. Perhaps further study on a return of a stronger metropolitan structure, especially since it is still central to our Eastern brothers and sisters, would be helpful. Finally, further study and ritual expression of the role of the unitive function of the Bishop of Rome, successor of Peter, as the one called to confirm his brothers in the governance of the Church would be helpful.

The final, and perhaps most basic, issue is that of the need for maturity in living out obedience. A commitment to obedience can only come out of a certain level of maturity and then lead to a fuller level of maturity as sons and daughters of God. Much more study needs to be done on the issue of maturity in spiritual formation of those petitioning for orders and on the issue of the maturity of those entrusted with leadership in the Church and to whom obedience is promised. Only then will the ritual expressions in the rites of ordination, whereby a deacon or presbyter promises obedience and reverence to his bishop or a bishop faithfully exhibits obedience to the pope, be true and meaningful symbols of the reality they manifest.

It is in this final context that we can ask the final question. Should a public promise of obedience be part of the rites of ordination? Promises of obedience are not intrinsic to rites of ordination. However, the importance of such a public commitment seems evident in a world such as ours. Nevertheless, as in all commitments, obedience can only be ritualized in a context that is reciprocal, mutual, and freeing. While the words and gestures of such a ritual would be important, more important would be the level of Christian maturity lived by both parties, the one making the promise of obedience and the one to whom the promise is made. Thus, we return to our image of the obedience of Christ, who, while obedient even to death, trusted that the Father would hear him. May we enter more deeply into that obedience which, while an entrance into death to self, leads to the fullness of new life in Christ.

Bibliography

SOURCES

Acta Synodalia Sacrosancti Concilii Oecumenici Vaticani Secundi. 4 vols. Rome, 1970–83.

Andrieu, M, ed. *Le Pontifical Romain au Moyen-Âge.* 4 vols. Città del Vaticano, 1938–41.

   Tome 1. *Le Pontifical Romain du XII siècle.* 1938.

   Tome 2. *Le Pontifical de la Curie Romaine au XIII siècle.* 1940.

   Tome 3. *Le Pontifical de Guillaume Durand.* 1940.

———, ed. *Les Ordines romani du haut moyen âge.* Vols. 3 and 4. Louvain, 1931–61.

Caspar, E. *Das Register Gregors VII.* Berlin, 1920–3.

Catalanus, J. *Pontificale Romanum.* 3 vols. Paris, 1850.

Code of Canons of the Eastern Churches. Latin-English edition. Washington, D.C.: Canon Law Society of America, 1992.

Code of Canon Law. Latin-English edition. Washington, D.C.: Canon Law Society of America, 1983.

De Ordinatione Diaconi, Presbyteri et Episcopi. Editio Typica. Typis Polyglottis Vaticanis, 1968.

De Ordinatione Episcopi, Presbyterorum et Diaconorum. Editio Typica Altera. Typis Polyglottis Vaticanis, 1990.

de Vogüé, A. "La Règle de Saint Benoît." *Sources Chretiennes* 181, 184, 186. Paris: Les Éditions du Cerf, 1972.

Friedburg, E., ed. *Gratianus (Decretum) Corpus Iuris Canonici.* Vol. 1. Graz: Akademische Druck and Verlagsanstalt, 1959. Reprint of 1879 edition.

Hanslik, R., ed. "Benedicti Regula," *Corpus Scriptorum Ecclesiasticorum Latinorum* 75. Vienna, 1960.

Holste, L. *Codex Regularum Monasticarum et Canonicarum.* 1759. Reprint Graz, 1958.

Lentini, A. *S. Benedetto: La Regola.* Monte Casino, 1980.

Mansi, J. D. *Sacrorum Conciliorum: Nova et Amplissima Collectio.* Vol. 2. Reprint: Graz, 1960.

Martène, E. *De Antiquis Ecclesiae Ritibus Libri.* 4 vols. 1736. Reprint: Hildesheim, 1967.

Migne, J. P. *Patrologiae Cursus Completus, series Latina.* Vol. 89; Boniface. Vols. 125–6, Hincmar.

Mittermüller, R., ed. *Vita et Regula Ss. P. Benedicti una cum Expositione Regulae.* Regensburg, 1880.

Mohlberg, L., ed. *Sacramentarium Veronense.* Herder: Rome, 1978.

Munier, C., ed. *Les Statuta Ecclesiae Antiqua. Édition-Études critiques.* Strasbourg, 1960.

Nabuco, J., *Pontificalis Romani.* Vol. 1. New York: Benziger, 1945.

Ordo Benedictionis Abbatis et Abbatissae. Editio Typica. Typis Polyglottis Vaticanis, 1978.

Ordo Professionis Religiosae. Editio Typica. Typis Polyglottis Vaticanis, 1970.

Paul VI. "Ecclesiae Sanctae." *Acta Apostolicae Sedis* 58 (1966) 757–75.

Paulus Warnefridus. *In Sanctam Regulam Commentarium ad XIV saeculorum ss. Benedicti nativitatis annum.* Monte Cassino, 1880.

Pius XII. "Cleri Sanctitati." *Acta Apostolicae Sedis* 49 (1957) 433–603.

Pontificale Romanum. Pars Prima. Editio typica. Typis Polyglottis Vaticanis, 1962.

Sancrosanctum Oecumenicum Concilium Vaticanum II. Città del Vaticano, 1966.

Spannagel, A., and P. Engelbert, eds. *Corpus Consuetudinum Monasticarum 8.* Siegburg, 1974.

Tanner, N., ed. *Decrees of the Ecumenical Councils.* Vols. 1 and 2. London: Sheed & Ward Ltd., 1990.

Vogel, C., ed. *Le Pontifical Romano-Germanique du Dixième Siècle.* Vol. 1. Città del Vaticano, 1963.

ARTICLES AND STUDIES

Alberigo, G. *Lo sviluppo della dottrina sui poteri nella Chiesa universale: Momenti essenziali tra il XVI e il XIX secolo.* Rome: Herder, 1964.

Alberigo, G., and A. Weiler, eds. *Election and Consensus in the Church.* Concilium 77. Herder & Herder, 1972.

Andrieu, M. "La carrière ecclésiastique des Papes et les documents liturgiques du Moyen Âge." *Revue des Sciences Religieuses* 21 (1947) 91–120.

Aubry, A. "A propos de la signification du <<Promitto>>." *Nouvelle Revue Theologique* 85 (1963) 1063–8.

Augustine, C. *A Commentary on the New Code of Canon Law.* Vols. 2 and 6. London: Herder, 1936.

Berbig, H. "Zur rechtlichen Relevanz von Ritus und Zeremoniell im römisch-deutschen Imperium." *Zeitschrift für Kirchengeschichte* 92 (1981) 204–49.

Betti, U. "'Professio Fidei' et 'Iusiurandum Fidelitatis.'" *Notitiae* 25 (1989) 319–25.

Beyer, J. "Nature et Position du Sacerdoce." *Nouvelle Revue Theologique* 76 (1954) 356–73.

Bihlmeyer, K., and H. Tüchle. *Church History.* 3 vols. Paderborn: F. Schöningh, 1963.

Blaise, A. *Lexicon Latinitatis Medii Aevi.* Turnholti: Brepols, 1975.

Böckman, A. "RB5: Benedict's Chapter on Obedience." *American Benedictine Review* 45 (1994) 109–30.

Botte, B. "Collegiate Character of the Presbyterate and Episcopate." *The Sacrament of Orders.* Collegeville: The Liturgical Press (1962) 73–97.

―――. "L'Ordination de L'Évêque." *La Maison-Dieu* 98 (1969) 113–26.

Bouscaren, L. *The Canon Law Digest.* Milwaukee: Bruce Publishing Co., 1934.

Bradshaw, P. *Ordination Rites of the Ancient Churches of East and West.* Pueblo, 1990.

Brandolini, L. "L'evoluzione storica dei riti delle ordinazioni." *Ephemerides Liturgicae* 83 (1969) 67-87.

Braun, J. *Die liturgische Gewandung in Occident und Orient nach Ursprung und Entwicklung, Verwendung und Symbolik.* Freiburg (1907) 620–76.

Brooke, R. *The Coming of the Friars.* London: George Allen & Unwin Ltd, 1975.

Bugnini, A. *The Reform of the Liturgy.* Collegeville: The Liturgical Press, 1990.

Catella, A. "La liturgia romana al di qua e al di là delle Alpi." *Rivista Liturgica* 4–5 (1993) 443–62.

Chavasse, A. *La liturgie de la ville de Rome du V au VIII siécle* (Studia Anselmiana 112). Rome: S. Anselmo, 1993.

Chodorow, S. *Christian Political Theory and Church Politics in the Mid-Twelfth Century: The Ecclesiology of Gratian's Decretum.* University of California Press, 1972.

Chupungco, A. *Liturgical Inculturation: Sacramentals, Religiosity, and Catechesis.* Collegeville: The Liturgical Press, 1992.

Cnudde, M. "L'Ordination des Diacres." *La Maison-Dieu* 98 (1969) 73–94.

Collins, M. "The Public Language of Ministry." In J. Provost, ed., *Official Ministry in a New Age.* Canon Law Society of America (1981) 7–40. Reprinted in M. Collins. *Worship: Renewal to Practice.* The Pastoral Press (1987) 137–73.

Colombo, C. "La fonction de l'Épiscopat dans l'Église et ses relations avec la Primauté Pontificale." *Istina* 8 (1961) 7–32.

Congar, Y. "Faits, problèmes et reflexions à propos du pouvoir d'ordre et des rapports entre le presbytérat et l'épiscopat." *La Maison-Dieu* 14 (1948) 107–28.

―――. "Les ministères d'Église dans le monde féodal jusqu'à la réforme Grégorienne." *Revue de Droit Canonique* 23 (1973) 77–97.

Cooke, B. "'Fullness of Orders': Theological Reflections." In J. Provost, ed., *Official Ministry in a New Age.* Canon Law Society of America (1981) 151–67.

―――, ed. *The Papacy and the Church in the United States.* Paulist Press, 1989.

Coomaraswamy, R. "The Post-Conciliar Rite of Holy Orders." *Studies in Comparative Religion* 16 (1984) 154–87.

Cowan, M., ed. *Alternative Futures for Worship: Leadership Ministry in Community.* Vol. 6. Collegeville: The Liturgical Press, 1987.

de Aspurz, L. "Il rito della professione nell'ordine Francescano." *Studi Francescani* 66 (1969) 245–68.

Dell'Oro, F. "La 'Editio typica altera' del Pontificale Romano delle Ordinazioni." *Rivista Liturgica* 78 (1991) 281–335.

Faris, J. *Eastern Catholic Churches: Constitution and Governance.* New York: Saint Maron Publications, 1992.

Fox, J. P. "The Personal Prelature of the Second Vatican Council: An Historical Canonical Study." Rome: Diss. Angelicum, 1987.

Galmes, L. and V. Gomez. *Santo Domingo de Guzmán.* Madrid: BAC, 1987.

Galot, J. *Theology of the Priesthood.* San Francisco: Ignatius Press, 1985.

Gaudemet, J. "Holy Orders in Early Conciliar Legislation." *The Sacrament of Orders.* Collegeville: The Liturgical Press (1962) 182–201.

Giraldo, R. *Problematica sul Rapporto tra Poteri Papali e Consacrazione Episcopale.* Vicenza, 1978.

Huizing, P., and K. Walf, eds. *Electing Our Own Bishops.* Concilium 137. Seabury Press, 1980.

Jedin, H., ed. *Handbook of Church History.* 10 vols. New York: Herder & Herder, 1969.

———. "Zur Theologie der Episkopates von Trindentinum bis zum Vaticanum I." *Trierer Theologische Zeitschrift* 74 (1965) 176–81.

Jedin, H., and G. Alberigo. *Il Typo Ideale di Vescovo secundo la Riforma Cattolica.* Brescia: Morcelliana, 1985.

Joncas, M. "New Roman Rite Prayer of Ordination of Presbyters." *The Priest* 48 (1992) 39–47.

———. "Recommendations Concerning Roman Rite Ordinations Leading to the Reform Mandated in Sacrosanctum Concilium 76," *Ecclesia Orans* 9 (1992) 307–40.

———. "The Public Language of Ministry Revisited: De Ordinatione Episcopi, Presbyterorum et Diaconorum." *Worship* 68 (1994) 386–403.

Jounel, P. "La Nouvelle Édition Typique du Rituel des Ordinations." *La Maison-Dieu* 186 (1991) 7–22.

———. "Le Nouveau Rituel D'Ordination." *La Maison-Dieu* 98 (1969) 63–72.

———. "Ordinations." *The Church at Prayer.* Vol. 3. Collegeville: The Liturgical Press (1987) 139–79.

Kaczynski, R. "Ein neues Pontifikale für die katholischen Bistümer des deutschen Sprachgebietes." *Liturgisches Jahrbuch* 43 (1993) 223–63.

Kleinheyer, B. "Chrismamesse oder Erneuerung der priesterlichen Versprechen? Ein Blick in die neuen und neuesten liturgischen Bücher." *Liturgisches Jahrbuch* 22 (1972) 1–17.

———. *Die Priesterweihe im Römischen Ritus* (Trierer Theologische Studien 12) Trier, 1962.

———. "L'Ordination de Prêtres." *La Maison-Dieu* 98 (1969) 95–112.

———. "Ordinationen und Beauftragungen." *Gottesdienst der Kirche: Handbuch der Liturgiewissenschaft.* Teil 8, Regensburg (1984) 12–65.

———. "Ordinationsfeiern." *Liturgisches Jahrbuch* 41 (1991) 88–118.

———. "Studien zur Nichtrömisch-Westlichen Ordinationsliturgie." *Archiv für Liturgiewissenschaft* 22 (1980) 93–107.

———. "Weiheliturgie in Neuer Gestalt." *Liturgisches Jahrbuch* 18 (1968) 210–29.

Knowles, D. *The Christian Centuries.* Vol. 2. London: Darton, Longman & Todd, 1969.

Khoury, J. "The Election of Bishops in the Eastern Churches." In P. Huizing and K. Walf, eds., *The Revised Code of Canon Law: A Missed Opportunity?* Concilium 147. Seabury Press, (1981) 20–7.

Lecuyer, J. "Commentarium." *Notitae* 4 (1968) 213–9.

Leroquais, V. *Les Pontificaux.* 3 vols. Paris, 1937.

Lessi-Ariosto, M. "Commentarium." *Notitae* 26 (1990) 95–115.

Lodi, E. *Enchiridion Euchologicum Fontium Liturgicorum.* Roma: Edizioni Liturgiche, 1979.

Martimort, A. G. *La Documentation liturgique de Dom Edmond Martène, SeT 279.* Citta del Vaticano, 1978.

Martos, J. *Doors to the Sacred.* New York: Doubleday, 1981.

Metz, R. "La désignation des évêques dans le droit actuel: étude comparative entre le Code latin de 1983 et le Code oriental de 1990." *Studia Canonica* 27 (1993) 321–34.

Mohrmann, C. "La langue de Saint Benoît." *Études sur le Latin des Chretiens.* Vol. 2, Rome, 1961.

Müller, A. "Obedience to the Bishop." In E. Schillebeeckx, ed., *The Unifying Role of the Bishop.* Concilium 71, Herder & Herder (1972) 79–88.

Munier, C. "Nouvelles recherches sur les 'Statuta ecclesiae antique.'" *Revue de Droit Canonique* 9 (1959) 170–80. Reprinted in Charles Munier, *Vie conciliaire et collections canonique en Occident IV-XII siècle.* London: Variorum Reprints, 1987.

———. "Une forme abrégeé du rituel d'ordination des 'Statuta ecclesiae antique.'" *Revue des Sciences Religieuses* 32 (1958) 79–84.

Nichols, A. *Holy Orders.* Dublin: Veritas, 1990.

O'Malley, J. W. "Priesthood, Ministry, and Religious Life: Some Historical and Historiographical Considerations." *Theological Studies* 49 (1988) 223–57.

Orsy, L. "Bishops, Presbyters, and Priesthood in Gratian's 'Decretum.'" *Gregorianum* 44 (1963) 788–826.

Osborne, K. *Priesthood: A History of Ordained Ministry in the Roman Catholic Church.* New York: Paulist Press, 1988.

Pastor, L. *History of the Popes.* Vols. 17 and 24. London, 1951.

Pospishil, V. *Code of Oriental Canon Law: The Law on Persons.* Philadelphia: America, 1960.

———. *Eastern Catholic Church Law.* New York: St. Maron Publications, 1993.

Power, D. *Ministers of Christ and His Church.* London: Chapman, 1969.

———. "The Basis for Official Ministry in the Church." In J. Provost, ed., *Official Ministry in a New Age.* Canon Law Society of America (1981) 60–88.

———. *The Eucharistic Mystery: Revitalizing the Tradition.* New York: Crossroad, 1992.

Provost, J., ed. *Official Ministry in a New Age.* Canon Law Society of America, 1981.

Pulickal, T. "A Study of the Rite of Religious Profession and its Adaptation to the Cultural Traditions of India." Rome: Diss. S. Anselmo, 1991.

Rado, P. *Enchiridion Liturgicum.* Vol. 2. Rome: Herder (1961) 958–1034.

Ramstein, M. *A Manual of Canon Law.* Hoboken N.J.: Terminal Publishing Co., 1948.

Rouillard, P. "Ministères et ordination en occident." *Il Ministero Ordinato Nel Dialogo Ecumenico* (Studia Anselmiana 92). Rome: S. Anselmo (1985) 107-24.

Russo, R. "La MISSA CRISMAL: un <<propio>> que exige grandes cambios." *Ecclesia Orans* 10 (1993) 201-29.

Ryan, S. "Episcopal Consecration: The Fullness of the Sacrament of Order." *Irish Theological Quarterly* 32 (1965) 293-324.

———. "Episcopal Consecration: The Legacy of the Schoolmen." *Irish Theological Quarterly* 33 (1966) 3–38.

———. "Episcopal Consecration: Trent to Vatican II," *Irish Theological Quarterly* 33 (1966) 133–50.

———. "Vatican II: The Rediscovery of the Episcopate." *Irish Theological Quarterly* 33 (1966) 208–41.

Salmon, P. *Etude sur Les Insignes du Pontife dans Le Rit Romain.* Roma: Officium Libri Catholici, 1955.

Santantoni, A. *L'Ordinazione Episcopale* (Studia Anselmiana 69) Rome: S. Anselmo, 1976.

Schillebeeckx, E. *Ministry.* New York: Crossroad, 1981.

———. *The Church with a Human Face.* New York: Crossroad, 1985.

———, ed. *The Unifying Role of the Bishop.* Concilium 71. Herder & Herder, 1972.

Schneider, F. "Obedience to the Bishop by the Diocesan Priest in the 1983 Code of Canon Law." Washington, D.C.: Diss. Catholic University of America, 1990.

Seasoltz, K. "Religious Obedience: Liberty and Law." In P. Philibert, ed., *Living in the Meantime.* Paulist Press (1994) 73–93.

Sweeney, G. "The 'Wound in the Right Foot': Unhealed?" In A. Hastings, ed., *Bishops and Writers.* Anthony Clarke Books (1977) 207–34.

Tavard, G. H. "Episcopacy and Apostolic Succession According to Hincmar of Reims." *Theological Studies* 34 (1973) 594–623.

Thomas, A. "La profession religieuse des Dominicains." *Archivum Fratrum Praedicatorum* 39 (1969) 5–52.

Vogel, C. *Medieval Liturgy: An Introduction to the Sources.* Washington, D.C.: The Pastoral Press, 1986.

———. "Titre d'ordination et lien du presbytre à la communauté locale dans l'Église ancienne." *La Maison-Dieu* 115 (1973) 70–85.

Vorgrimler, H., ed. *Commentary on the Documents of Vatican II.* Vols. 1–5. New York: Herder & Herder, 1969.

Woywod, S. *A Practical Commentary on the Code of Canon Law.* New York: Joseph Wagner, Inc., 1957.

Yeo, R. *The Structure and Context of Monastic Profession* (Studia Anselmiana 83). Rome: S. Anselmo, 1982.